A TIME
TO ACT

Archibald MacLeish

A TIME

TO ACT

★ ★ *Selected Addresses* ★ ★

BOSTON 1943

HOUGHTON MIFFLIN COMPANY

BOOKS BY
ARCHIBALD MacLEISH

The Happy Marriage
The Pot of Earth
Nobodaddy
Streets in the Moon
The Hamlet of A. MacLeish
New Found Land
Conquistador
Frescoes for Mr. Rockefeller's City
Poems
Panic
Public Speech
The Fall of the City
Land of the Free
Air Raid
America Was Promises
The Irresponsibles
The American Cause
A Time to Speak
A Time to Act

Nov. 1958

The Riverside Press
CAMBRIDGE · MASSACHUSETTS
PRINTED IN THE U.S.A.

Acknowledgments

GRATEFUL ACKNOWLEDGMENT is made to Duell, Sloan and Pearce, Inc., for permission to use 'The American Cause'; to *The Nation* for 'To the Class of 1941'; to *The Yale Review* for 'The Problem of the New World' (originally published under the title 'The American Writers'); and to *The Atlantic Monthly* for 'Colloquy for the States,' 'The Image of Victory,' and for 'Prophets of Disaster,' reprinted by the University of Pennsylvania Press under the title of 'Prophets of Doom.'

Contents

COLLOQUY FOR THE STATES

A Poem

★
★
★
★

Colloquy for the States

THERE'S TALK *says Illinois.*
                    Is there says Iowa.
There's talk on the east wind says Illinois.

Talk about what says Dakota says Kansas says Arkansas.

Can't make out: too far east says Michigan.

East of the roosters says Indiana.
                    East of the
Morning crows says Ohio.
                    East says York State.

East still says Connecticut: on east.

It's down east from here says Massachusetts.

It's east of the Quoddy says Maine but I hear it.
                                        Hear

What says Texas.
              What can you hear says Virginia.
Can't be sure says Maine.   Surf on the reefs.
Ice pounding away on the pans in Penobscot.

Listen says Oregon.
              Scoop your ear says Kentucky.

Can't tell says Maine.   Too much fog.
Bells on the Old Orchard.   Horns at Ogunquit.

Listen says Mississippi.
              Try to says Texas.
Lean your lug to the loo'ard says Massachusetts.

It's tall talk says Maine.   It's tall talking —
Tall as a calf in a fog.
              Call it says Arkansas.
It's mean talk says Maine.   It's mouthy meaning.

Mean about what says Nebraska.
              Mean about us.
What about us says Kentucky says Texas says Idaho.

I gather they don't like us says Maine.
                                        Do
Tell says Connecticut.
              I vum says New Hampshire.
I gather we've low ways says Maine.
                                        That
So says Kansas.

Take my seat says Michigan.

It's how we marry says Maine. We ain't choosers.
We scrabble them up and we mingle them in. We
    marry the
Irish girls with the shoes with the quick come-after.
We marry the Spaniards with the evening eyes.
We marry the English with the tiptoe faces.
We marry the golden Swedes: the black Italians:
The German girls with the thick knees: the Mex-
    icans
Lean and light in the sun with the jingling and jang-
    ling:
The Chileñas for luck: the Jews for remembrance: the
    Scots girls
Tall as a tall man — silver as salmon;
The French with the skillful fingers: the long loves.
I gather we marry too many says Maine: too various.
I gather we're bad blood: we're mixed people.

That's what they say says Texas.
            That's what they're saying.
What's in their soup says Arkansas: what they been
    eating?

What's in their hair says Maryland.
            Aren't they men:
Can't they make it with strangers says Alabama.

Are they shy says Missouri.
            Or what says Montana.

I gather they're
Bred pure says Maine: they're superior people.

Have they seen our kids says York State: the tall girls
The small elegant breasts they have like Egyptians
The long legs with the delicate slender bones
And the wrists supple and small as a man's three fingers —
The way they walk on the world with their narrow
*   heels?*
You can tell them anywhere: tell them in any country —
The height of their heads and the tilt of their heels
*   when they walk.*
A head higher than most: a hand smaller.

Have they raced our boys says Michigan — fast as black
*   snakes:*
Quick on the gun as quail: the sweet striders:
The watchful lads in the lead: dangerous followers:
Strong hearts in the stretch home.   Have they beaten
*   them?*

I gather they haven't says Maine.   I gather we're mixed
Bloods: they don't take to us.
*   Don't they says Kansas.*
Have they seen our towns says Kansas: seen our wheat:
Seen our flatcars in the Rocky Mountains:
Seen our four-lane highways: seen our planes
Silver over the Alleghenies the Lakes
The big timber the tall corn the horses —
Silver over the snow-line: over the surf?

Have they seen our farms says Kansas: and who plowed
    them?
Have they seen our towns says Kansas: and who planned
    them?

Have they seen our men says Kansas.
                         Gather not:
Gather we're bad blood says Maine.   They're saying so.

Who says says Missouri: who's this saying?

Where from says Montana: where's he from?

Where from: who says Georgia.
                       Can't make out.
Way east: east of the Rhine it might be.
The wind veers says Maine.   I don't make out.

East of the Rhine: so that's it says Montana.

The pure-bloods by the Rhine says Carolina.

The blood we left behind us says Wisconsin.

The blood we left behind us when we left:
The blood afraid of travel says Nevada.

The blood afraid of changes says Kentucky.

The blood afraid of strangers says Vermont: —

Strange stars and strange women: the two of them.

The blood that never hankered for a strange one: —
A dark one says Dakota with strange hair.

Stayed home and married their kin says Missouri.

Married their cousins who looked like their mothers
        says Michigan.

So that's all: east of the Rhine says Wisconsin.

So that's all says Arkansas: all for that —
All for the pure-bred boys afraid of strangers.

Surf on the reefs says Maine: ice on Penobscot . . .

There's talk says Iowa.
           Talk says Illinois.

Bells on the Old Orchard: bells at Ogunquit . . .

Clash of corn in the wind says Illinois.

THE RESPONSIBILITY OF THE PRESS

★

★

★

*

The Responsibility of the Press

ADDRESS DELIVERED BEFORE THE
AMERICAN SOCIETY OF NEWS-
PAPER EDITORS, APRIL 17, 1942

WHATEVER THE PRESS may have been in the life of any
other country, its significance in the present peril of
this republic is obvious.   Indeed, if you include with
the American press the other great instruments of
American enlightenment, it is no more than the sober
truth to say that those instruments constitute together
the principal American weapon in this war.

It has been frequently said, but it has not been altogether believed even by those who have said it most,
that the real battlefield of this war is the field of
American opinion.   And yet it is true – and no one

knows it better than our enemies. It is their principal hope that they can so divide and confuse and demoralize American opinion that the American determination to fight the war through to an ultimate victory will fail of itself regardless of the resources of American men and American machines which, backed by American will, would make an ultimate victory certain. It is our principal hope, on our side, that we can so unite and inform and hearten American opinion that the American determination to win will survive any conceivable disaster abroad and any possible propaganda of treachery and fraud at home.

That hope is a hope the citizens of this country confide primarily to the press: to the great traditional instruments of communication and of information — the press, the radio, and the moving pictures. It is traditionally to its press, its parsons, its professors, and its poets — and approximately in that order — that the people of this country turn for counsel in the difficult and dangerous business of making up their minds. Needless to say the American people do not always take the advice of any of them. But no one I think will seriously question the proposition that, over the course of the republic's history, the press has played a larger part than any other instrument in shaping the public, as distinguished from the private, mind.

Certainly it has played a larger part than government. Under the American system it is not the government which shapes the public mind but the public mind which shapes the government. Government officials, executive as well as legislative, may argue in their in-

dividual capacities for their individual beliefs like any
other citizens, but the American theory is that government itself should not exercise that function. The duty
of government has been assumed to be the duty of re-
porting to the people any facts in its possession which
the people might require to enable them to reach a
sound judgment and an informed opinion. But under
the American theory, government itself has not been
considered to be charged with responsibility for the
formation of the opinions of the people. That responsibility in our system has been charged primarily to the
people themselves, and thereafter to those who undertake to influence the people's judgments. Of these the
directors of the press, historically and in length of influence, stand first.

That this American system presents certain difficulties, no one who has given the matter any thought
will doubt. One difficulty is the difficulty of drawing
the precise line between the duty of government to
report to the people and the function of the press. The
press, in the first few months of this war, as throughout
the last, has evidenced a very considerable uneasiness
on that subject. Its criticism of the government information services reflects in part at least its genuine concern about the relation of its functions to the information functions of the government.

The essence of the difficulty is, as I see it, that there
is no clear agreement as to the relative *responsibilities*
of government and press. A workable division of any
function can only be made if there is also an agreed
division of responsibility. But it is precisely in the

matter of responsibility that no agreement exists. The traditional American theory that government has no responsibility for the formation of opinion is not balanced by any comparable view as to the responsibility of the press. Specifically it is not balanced by any comparable view as to the responsibility of the press as a whole for the opinion-influencing activities of its various members.

This country is engaged in war. Its situation in that war is perilous. And nevertheless there are minority elements of the American press which are actively engaged in influencing American opinion in directions which lead not to victory but to defeat. There are, in other words, elements of the American press, claiming the same right to influence American opinion as is claimed by the majority, who, even at this moment of national peril, are engaged in an attempt to influence American opinion in a direction opposite to the direction of the majority of the press, opposite to the direction of the government, and opposite to the direction which leads to a victorious conclusion of this war.

The question which presents itself is therefore this: whose is the responsibility — government or press? What do those of us in government and press who mean to win this war propose to do about it? Whose is the responsibility for action — yours or ours?

There are plenty of people who will tell you that the responsibility is government's — that government, through its law-enforcement agencies, should crack down — should suppress all publications of this divisive and defeatist nature. I don't believe it. And neither,

I think, do you. Government will crack down where there is a violation of law. But the most poisonous and pervasive defeatism is not practiced by those who violate the statutes of their country openly. It is practiced by those who take scrupulous care to stay within the law — to come, as one of them is reported to have told his staff, 'as close to treason as I dare.' To silence publishers and editors such as those by criminal prosecution would inevitably endanger the freedom of the honest editor and the loyal publisher. The defeatists and the divisionists who strike from that ambiguous and doubtful shadow where freedom of expression darkens into treason cannot be hunted out by the police without the risk of injury to rights that must on no account be injured. The weapon which reaches them — the one weapon with which they can safely be hunted — is the weapon they themselves employ: the weapon of the word.

But those of us who take that view must decide for ourselves to what conclusions it leads us. If the responsibility is not the government's, is it then the duty of the loyal and honest press to hunt out and to expose by every instrument of truth the skulkers in the journalistic ambush — the cowardly, half-hearted publishers, and the venal editors of their staffs, who use for their own disloyal purposes the cover of the noblest right that free men boast of — the right to speak your mind according to your conscience in despite of hell?

I think many of you — very many of you — would say the answer to that question, in the interest of the press as well as in the interest of the country, must be, Yes —

and that the past practice in this regard must now be
altered. For certainly the past practice of the profession has been otherwise. The reasons are understood and understandable. Journalists dislike self-
righteousness as much as or more than any men. And
in ordinary times it was assumed that such aberrations
would take care of themselves — that the wages of sin
were loss of circulation.

But for whatever reason, the profession of the press
has not traditionally policed its members. Newspapers
guilty of the most flagrant crimes against the republic
have not been punished by their kind. Indeed newspaper editors alone among the citizens of the country
seem to have enjoyed immunity from newspaper attack
— a circumstance which has not failed to reach the
notice of the people. When a powerful newspaper-
owner can publish without criticism from his colleagues
a secret document of vital importance to the security of
his country — a document which could not have issued
from its place of safe-keeping by any but dishonorable
means — people of ordinary common sense and common
observation are inclined to wonder why. I think it is
no secret that they still are wondering.

More recently — within the last few weeks — there has
been a hopeful change. Newspapers of New York have
attacked editorially the defeatism and divisionism of
certain of their colleagues. Papers elsewhere have
turned the floodlights of truthful information upon the
contemptible little Jew-baiting, Roosevelt-hating rags of
the fascist fringe. Magazines have published explicit
accounts of the activities of the worst of the divisionists

and defeatists. But these cleansing operations have thus far been sporadic and occasional. As long as continuing and persistent efforts are made by a small minority of the press, without rebuke from the vast majority of the press, to weaken the American determination to win, to divide the American people from their desperately needed allies, and even to corrupt the confidence of the American people in their government and in themselves, it can hardly be said that the press as a whole has accepted the responsibility it must accept if the press is to police itself.

It will be replied, I know, that the distinction between democratic criticism and defeatist propaganda is difficult to draw and that the press must be vigilant to defend the right of criticism everywhere in order that it may be curtailed nowhere. No one questions — no one so far as I know has ever questioned — the necessity of criticism in a democracy. Criticism of the administration of affairs is essential to the health of a democracy and never more so than in time of war. It should not be limited in any free man's country and certainly it has not been limited in this: a more consistently critical press than the American press of the last three months would be hard to imagine. The press is justified in defending its right to criticize, and should and must defend it at all costs.

But the necessity of defending the right of democratic criticism does not absolve any man in time of war from distinguishing between democratic criticism and defeatist propaganda disguised as criticism. It is merely irresponsible to say, as certain journals and journalists have

in effect said recently, that anyone who objects that defeatist criticism is helpful to the enemy is objecting that
all criticism is helpful to the enemy and is therefore
attempting to suppress all criticism. It is an easy reply
but it is not, if you will forgive me, an intellectually
honest reply. There is a very clear distinction between
criticism aimed to support the will to win this war and
criticism aimed to defeat that will. And criticism
aimed to defeat it is in simple fact helpful — extremely
helpful — to our enemies. To draw attention to that
fact is not an attack upon the freedom of the press. It
is a duty, if an outsider may say so, owed by honest
journalism to the republic. The journalist who refuses
to perform that duty himself and who rebukes those
who attempt to perform it in his place has not, I think,
increased the fame of his profession.

There can, for example, be no question in any mind
but that the sole purpose of newspaper propaganda
aimed to divide our people from the Russian people or
the British people at this moment of real and present
danger, is defeatist. If successful this propaganda can
have no possible effect but to weaken us in a struggle
in which we desperately need every strength, every aid,
we can muster. There can equally be no question but
that the sole purpose of newspaper propaganda aimed
to inspire a demand for a defensive war, a war for the
defense of our own coasts and our own islands, a with-
drawal of our forces for our own defense, is defeatist.
If successful this propaganda also can have no possible
effect but to destroy our will to fight, leaving us de-
fenseless against the peace offensive our enemies are

certain to launch. Indeed the most obvious purpose of this propaganda is precisely to prepare us to lose the war by a negotiated 'peace.' Equally again there can be no question but that the sole purpose of newspaper propaganda calculated to inflame race against race or class against class or group against group is defeatist. If successful this propaganda would divide us internally precisely as our enemies propose we shall be divided. But all these forms of propaganda are practiced, nevertheless, by minority elements of the American press and practiced for the most part without rebuke from the press as a whole.

The real question, as I see it, then, is this: Will the American press as an American institution accept, *with all their implications,* the responsibilities which accompany the functions it has exercised so long, so courageously, and so well? Will it accept, as a consequence of its traditional right to influence American opinion, a responsibility for the opinion which results? Will it accept that responsibility not only against the open propagandists of the Axis but against those of its own membership who follow, consciously or unconsciously, the Axis lead?

There was a time when the chief and almost the only concern of a free press in a free country was to protect its freedom against the encroachments of its own government. I think you will agree that a part of the American press acts today as though we still lived in that time — as though our freedoms were secure and our battles were won if only the government could be kept from encroaching on the preserves of the press

either negatively by suppression or affirmatively by publications of its own.   But unfortunately for us all we do
not live in such a simple and idyllic age.   Unfortunately
for us all we live in a doubtful and shadowy world of
fascist conspiracy and fraud in which, not only the freedom of the press, but freedom itself is endangered by
the employment against us of the very instruments of
freedom, the instruments of information and enlightenment themselves, and not least the press.   In such a
world it is not enough for any man, journalist or other,
to fight for the freedom of ideas.   It is necessary now to
fight for the idea of freedom.   It is not enough to claim
the right to influence opinion.   It is necessary to accept
responsibility for the opinions which result.

This responsibility the best of the American press has
already accepted both in word and practice.   The best
of the American press is at one with the great majority
of the American people in the determination that this
war shall be won at any cost and in the face of any
suffering and any danger.   The best of the American
press is determined to win the battle for American
opinion against any propaganda from abroad or treason
from within — even treason in its own ranks and among
its own members.   If the press as a whole will accept
that purpose and the burden that goes with it, there will
be forged in the United States a firmness of resolve, a
sharpness of resolution, which nothing that our enemies
can bring against us by force, or fear or fraud can ever
break.

THE STRATEGY OF TRUTH

★
★
★
★

The Strategy of Truth

ADDRESS DELIVERED AT THE AN-
NUAL LUNCHEON OF THE ASSO-
CIATED PRESS, APRIL 20, 1942

IT WOULD BE a gross distortion of the truth for me to
say, as is customary on these occasions, that it is a
pleasure to address you. Pleasure is a totally inadequate word. There is no man living — certainly there
is no man who does his living in public — who would
not jump at the chance. To have the masters of the
American press silenced in front of you for twenty
minutes while *you* tell *them,* is something any public
servant would gladly sacrifice his hope of heaven to
achieve.

You may realize that the silence is only temporary.

You may foresee, with complete clairvoyance, that a publisher from Chicago, say, and another from New York (to say nothing of their sisters and their cousins and their aunts in other cities) will turn the dogs on you in the morning papers. But nothing — not even the dread of being called a poet by those who do not care for poets — would induce you to decline. Discretion is the better part of valor only when you hope to have the chance to fight again. And the Lord alone knows when the Director of the Office of Facts and Figures will have another chance to talk back to the Associated Press.

That, however, is only part of the explanation. The rest of it is the simple but compelling fact that I have a question to ask you. The question is this:

You are aware — you are far better aware than I — that an Axis offensive on the psychological front is in the making. You have read the short-wave broadcasts from Vichy which quote Ankara as quoting 'neutral sources' as saying that Axis leaders are drafting proposals for a generous peace. You have heard the stories alleged to emanate from Switzerland to the effect that Goering is trying desperately to find an American to whom he can communicate the peaceful intentions of the Nazis.

The stories are doubtful, but their purpose isn't — at least to you. You have realized for a long time — for a far longer time than most of us — that an Axis 'peace' offensive is certain, sooner rather than later, to appear. These stories and others like them are the straws in the treacherous wind. And the question is, What are we

going to do about it? How are we — and by 'we' I
mean those of us in government and in the press who
are charged with certain responsibilities in this regard —
how are we going to prepare the people of the United
States to meet this danger? How are we going to warn
them of the nature and extent of the danger before it is
too late? And how, having warned them, are we going
to arm them to defend themselves against it?

I ask this question of you because it is, in the most
precise sense of the term, your business. A 'peace'
offensive is an offensive in political warfare, and political warfare is warfare fought with the weapons journalists and publishers are trained to use — the weapons of
ideas and words. It can be met and turned only by
the employment — by the most skillful and most effective employment — of these same weapons. And it is the
press, in a country which puts its reliance on a free and
independent press, which has that skill and can employ
it.

Government has its own responsibilities in these matters but government, under the American division of
responsibility as between the government and the press,
does not create, and does not therefore defend, American
opinion — does not, at least, defend it as long as the
traditional defenses provided by the press will stand.
For government to attempt to provide the country with
the services of information and warning and guidance
which the press can provide and has traditionally provided, would require an army of government information men beside which the present staffs of the government information services, however large they may look

from certain angles, would shrink to total insignificance.
Government, therefore, though it cannot avoid and
would certainly never wish to avoid, its full quota of
responsibility, is not the first or even the main line of
defense on this sector of the front. The first line is the
line held by your papers and the papers of your colleagues of the press, or the broadcasts of your colleagues
of the radio, and the duty of government, so long as that
line holds, is the duty of supporting your defenses.

The question of the strategy of the defense is therefore a question which presents itself to both of us but
first of all to you. It is not, I think you will agree, a
simple question. On the contrary, it is one of the most
difficult and complicated of all the questions presented
to this country by the present crisis. To begin with,
it is a novel question. Of political warfare, we, as a
people, have had little knowledge and even less experience. Politics we understand and have practiced, and
warfare we have had some expert knowledge of, but
political warfare is a different thing.

The people of our great cities can imagine with considerable accuracy what an air raid would be like and
are preparing themselves with intelligence and skill to
defend themselves against the danger. But a propaganda offensive — an attack not on their homes and on
their towns but on their hearts — they do not understand.

They use the word 'propaganda' readily enough.
They know that political warfare won victories in
France which dive bombers and flame-throwers and
tanks and parachute troops could never have won. But

the real and deadly danger of the weapons of political
warfare they do not realize, for these they have never
seen. We are a people to whom the most complicated
machines are understandable and the most incredible
mechanical miracles are believable, for we are familiar
with machines and we have practiced mechanical miracles. Bombers flying at impossible speeds and unat-
tainable heights are accepted without question and
observed without astonishment. But the devices of
psychological attack are another matter. Fraud as an
instrument of conquest is something we have read of
only, and the power of words to overthrow nations and
enslave their people is a power in which we do not
altogether or literally believe.

In a certain sense and to a certain degree that skepticism of our people is a source of strength, for it reflects
a confidence in our ability to see through tricks and
frauds which can be helpful. The American people,
whether Yankee by origin or not, have a fair sprinkling
of Yankee salt and Yankee humor, and salt and humor
are powerful preservatives of sanity and sense. But
there is a limit to the power of even the best of common
sense to protect a people.

The French were famous for their common sense
from one end of the earth to the other, and nevertheless
the French went down — and not least because of their
possession of that very quality. The Nazi propagandists
turned the famous common sense of the French people
against the people of France and from that moment the
cause of France was lost. When the soldiers of the
French armies and the workers in the French factories

began to ask themselves the 'common-sense' question
which the Nazi propagandists had put in their mouths —
Why are we fighting another war?   What will it get us?
Whom are we fighting for?   Why don't we just go home
and forget it?   What is there in it for us anyway? —
when the French peasants and their French soldiers began asking themselves these questions the war in France
was already over and the slavery of its people was prepared.

So that it would be a mistake to rely too heavily upon
the saving power of American common sense alone, or
to assume too easily that because the Americans do not
really believe in propaganda they will prove to be im-
mune to it.   Propaganda attacks upon the American
people will not come advertised as propaganda.   In so
far as our enemies are able to control them they will
come, or they will appear to come, as American suggestions originating within the United States.   We can
assume that our enemies, who have already demon-
strated a considerable skill in these matters, will control
their propaganda attack very well.

The question, then, of the strategy of national defense
upon this front presents itself with terrible insistence —
and presents itself primarily to those who, under the
American tradition in this matter, accept for themselves
certain responsibilities in the field of American opinion
— those who serve, and who control, the press.   In a
totalitarian country this responsibility would be a responsibility of government alone.   But we are waging
this war in order that America may remain a democratic
country — in order that America may achieve a greater,

not a narrower, democracy — and if the defense of American opinion against the new and formidable dangers of Nazi political warfare can be maintained by those who have maintained it against different dangers in the past, the responsibilities will continue to rest where they have rested.

What action the press should take through its various associations or otherwise, to determine this strategy of defense, it is not, of course, for outsiders to suggest. But even to the outsider it is evident that the question has two aspects — one internal to the press itself: a reorientation of the press to perform a wartime duty; and the other external: an organization of a method and a practice by which the press can meet successfully the attacks we now foresee.

The first of these problems I attempted to discuss a few days ago in addressing the American Society of Newspaper Editors at their convention here. Briefly, it seems to me, for whatever my opinion may be worth, that the press, in its own interest as well as in the national interest, must expose and counteract those of its members who, at this moment of national peril, are attempting to influence American opinion, not in the direction of American victory, but in the direction of American defeat. The press must police itself, not only to avoid necessity of a policing by government which neither government nor the press desires, but also to put itself in a position to perform the duties it has traditionally undertaken in American life.

That the American press will police itself to this end no man who knows the record of the American press

will doubt. Indeed the Augean labor has already been
begun. It can have but one possible termination. But
the cleansing of defeatists and divisionists will not alone
resolve the problem. It is not only necessary to deal
with those within the American press who weaken the
American will to win this war but with those also who attack it from without. Specifically, it is necessary to develop
and to perfect a strategy of defense against the devices
of political warfare which will insure the certain and
continuing defense of the republic on that front.

That strategy, I think, is neither difficult to find nor
difficult to name. It is the strategy which is appropriate
to our cause and to our purpose — the strategy of truth
— the strategy which opposes to the frauds and the deceits by which our enemies have confused and conquered other peoples the simple and clarifying truths
by which a nation such as ours must guide itself. But
the strategy of truth is not, because it deals in truth,
devoid of strategy. It is not enough, in this war of
hoaxes and delusions and perpetuated lies, to be merely
honest. It is necessary also to be wise. And, above all,
to be forearmed with wisdom.

The strategy of truth is peculiarly applicable therefore to the propaganda attack observers now foresee. To
prepare themselves against a 'peace' offensive, the
American people need to know what a Nazi peace
offensive is. They need to know, that is to say, that a
Nazi peace offensive is as much a Nazi weapon as a Nazi
mechanized division, or a fleet of Nazi planes. They
need to know in full the history of previous Nazi operations with this weapon. They need to know for what

purpose a Nazi peace offensive is made and with what end in view — that the end is never peace but always conquest — and that the inevitable consequence to the Nazi victims is defeat.

If the American people are informed in full of these purposes and these effects their defense will be assured. They will know how to deal with those who urge the talk of 'peace' upon them: and so whether it is proposed to them in terms of a negotiated 'peace' or in terms of a negotiated 'victory,' or in any other terms. For they will know then that the one peace possible to those who fight this war for freedom is the peace that free men make — and that the one victory conceivable to those who want their victory to serve the cause of freedom is the victory their courage and endurance win.

The strategy of truth, in other words, has for the object of its strategy a truthful understanding by the people of the meaning of the war in which they fight. Specifically, the strategy of truth has for object an understanding by the free peoples of the world that this war is a war in which no outcome but their victory can be conceivable. Defeat in this war is not possible in the sense in which defeat in other wars was possible — a defeat now to be followed by years of recuperation and a victory in a later war to follow. There will be no war to follow later if this war is lost. Those who win this war will see to it — and will see to it with relative ease — that the defeated will not fight a war for many years to come; will not have the means to fight a war; will not have the means to build the planes and tanks by which alone a modern war can be attempted. The defeated in this war will be defeated as the French are now defeated, as the Poles are now defeated, as the Danes are. No French Revolution of pitchforks against armies will be possible against the victors in this war; the fighting of the last two years has proven that.

That is one fact which the free peoples of the world must understand — the fact that this war is the last war those who love their freedom will ever have the chance to fight for freedom — if they lose.

The second fact is this: that negotiation in this war is not possible in the sense in which negotiation was possible in other wars. Knowing what we do or what we should of previous negotiations with the Axis Powers — negotiations in Munich, negotiations in the office of Secretary Hull while the Japanese planes were already over Honolulu — knowing this, none of those who now oppose the Axis would dare to trust the Axis in a negotiated peace, would dare relax one moment or disarm one regiment or return one factory to civil use as long as Hitler and the Japanese were armed and undefeated.

But these two facts equal, in the arithmetic of war, a third and final act, an ultimate conclusion: the conclusion that there is no possible outcome for the freedom-loving peoples in this war but a victory won by fighting, and that any proposal for any other outcome is a proposal which has for consequence, whatever may be pictured as its purpose, the defeat of freedom.

The ultimate objective of the strategy of truth is to carry to the people of this country, and the peoples who fight with them in this war, that certainty and understanding. For, once the true alternatives are clearly

seen and the necessary choice is firmly made, there can
be no question of the outcome of this war on any front
— either the front of arms and military effort, or the
front of purpose and opinion.

If the American press will devise defenses of this nature — if the American press will devote to the defense
of American opinion against the political warfare of our
enemies the intelligence, the imagination, the integrity,
the meticulous respect for accuracy, the devotion to the
truth which have characterized its practice of the profession of journalism at its best, there can be no question
but that the war upon the front of American opinion
will be won.

For we will then oppose to the propagandists of the
Axis powers a strategy of truth which the strategy of
fraud can never overcome and a wealth of talent and
of skill such as all the armies of the Nazi propaganda
offices could never hope to equal. No country has ever
had at its disposal greater resources with which to fight
the warfare of opinion than the practice of the profession of journalism in this country has produced. No
country will be more certain of the outcome of the war
if these resources, led by those who know them best, are
thrown into the struggle with conviction and with purpose — with unbreakable determination that nothing
but an absolute and final victory will suffice.

WE CANNOT ESCAPE HISTORY

★

★

★

★

We Cannot Escape History

ADDRESS DELIVERED BEFORE THE
CANADIAN CLUB AT OTTAWA, FEB-
RUARY 12, 1941

OTHERS IN OTHER COUNTRIES do not understand the American experience. They think of it not as an experience of men but as a discovery of land. They have read the names of the explorers and the roads by which they came — the inlets of the Rappahannock, the Florida beaches blinding with the surf, the Hudson narrowing into unknown hills and noblest of all, most beautiful of all, the clear St. Lawrence, fed by lakes as great as oceans, falling from the stone brim of the continent with a smoke and thunder of which no traveler who saw it ever ceased to speak. They know the names of

De Soto and Cabot and Hudson and Smith and Mackenzie and Cartier and La Salle and of the tribes of Indians and the rivers — the settlements at the head of navigation and at the places where the mountains could be passed. They know also the names of the cities we have built and the prairies we have fenced and the things we have done to this continent — some beautiful, some not beautiful.

But what they do not know and cannot know is the other side of this encounter. What they do not know and cannot know is the meaning of the American experience in the lives of the American peoples. Citizens of my country over many generations have used the word 'American' to mean themselves alone, but as the world narrows and the understanding of the hemisphere increases, it becomes evident even to the most proprietary among us that the word 'American' is not an exclusive but an inclusive title — one of the noblest of the earth's great names — a name belonging in common to all those who settled this continent — who came to it and saw it out of sea haze or at dusk or through the sunlight — those who chose it — those who chose to live here. America to the Americans — whether of British origin or French or Spanish — whether of our nation or yours or any other — was never a land only but a world — a new world — *the* new world. 'Nuevo Mundo Halló Colón,' reads the motto on the coat of arms of Columbus, and so in French and English also. A new world is not the same thing as a new land. A new land may be discovered. A new world must be created by the mind. A new land is earth and trees and water. A new world is a society of men.

Others in other countries have not understood this. They have thought of our attachment to liberty in the Americas, our concern for the dignity and self-respect of men, as a political formula, a byproduct of certain eighteenth-century developments in France, a philosophy imposed upon us by our reading or our thinking or our preachers. Our commitment to human freedom in the Americas is not of this origin. It is the consequence not of our philosophies but of our lives. We believe in human liberty and we believe in the moral order of the world, on which all confidence in human liberty must rest, not because high-minded persons have persuaded us of these things but because our life upon this continent has persuaded us.

The life that men have made in the vast American continent is a life they have made for themselves and separately, scattered over enormous distances where no writ ran and no authority of force alone could be effective — where men were held together only by their recognition and acceptance of some common good — where the life of men together was remitted therefore to its simplest and most universal sanctions: its common agreement at the common human level of decency and self-respect and consequent respect for others. If the Americans have confidence in personal liberty — confidence greater than their confidence in any other form of life in common — it is because the American experience has taught them to have confidence. If the peoples of this continent believe in the necessity of a moral order of the world on which their confidence in liberty may be rested, it is because they have good reason in their lives and in their history to believe this.

We know, we Americans — Canadians and citizens of the United States alike — we know, not by the instruction of books or by theoretical implication but by the American experience common to us both, that the basis of our lives upon this continent is a moral basis. We know by our own seeing, of our own knowledge, that the community of attachment which creates a nation in America is a community not of common race and blood, for there is no common race or blood, nor of common economic or material interest, for the economic and material interest is divided in itself, but only of attachment to a common principle — what Jefferson would have called a Proposition — an idea. We know that America, whatever it may seem to those who think of it as cities or as farms or mines or roads or grain or goods or metals, is in truth and in reality an idea. And that America — the idea which is America — the new world which was and is America — exists in the moral order of a moral world or nowhere.

'If the spirit of America were killed,' said Mr. Roosevelt, in an address which will not be forgotten — 'if the spirit of America were killed, even though the Nation's body and mind, constricted in an alien world, lived on, the America we know would have perished.'

Without the moral order of the world America is nothing — your nation as well as ours. Without it we are a hundred races and a score of religions and a multitude of interests sprawled across an enormous land, fenced beyond mountains, walled within valleys, separated by distances unthinkable to those who have not seen them. Without it we are another Europe with

another Europe's boundaries and divisions and a thousand more beside — boundaries and divisions drawn
across the wards and boroughs of a town, across the
village streets, the farmyard fences. With it, even the
boundary which separates your nation from our own is
less a separation than a meeting, for with you as with
ourselves a common respect for human dignity, a common attachment to the moral order, creates across the
geographical division of our nations a union of like-
minded men.

I say we know this, we Americans. But there are
some Americans who do not know it. There are some
in our day, as there were many in the time of Lincoln,
who do not understand the American experience; who
do not understand that America without the moral
order on which freedom rests is neither freedom nor
America; who deplore the raising of the moral issue
and the talk of freedom and of fascism — the talk of right
and wrong; who deplore it and denounce it as incite-
ment to a Holy War.

You know their voices. You have heard them here
as we have heard them — the voices which urge the
Americans to be realistic and to think of no one but
themselves and of nothing but their material advantage
— the voices which argue that American towns are too
far away for bombs to reach and therefore that falling
bombs mean nothing in America — the voices which tell
us that fascism will undoubtedly win in the end and that
it is useless therefore, and unwise beside, to say what
fascism is, or to give American aid to those who fight
against it, or even perhaps to fight to save ourselves —

the voices which tell us that the world will never be perfect; that we can't police the world; that we'll have to trade with the winners whoever they are; that the thing for us to do is to satisfy both and to anger neither — the voices which talk as the merchants were talking in Boston in '61 when J. M. Forbes wrote Sumner that they wanted 'a kind of compromise made that would promise to patch up difficulties and their pockets.'

They are scornful voices and cynical voices. They shout down all reminders that fascism is what all the world has learned it is. They tell us not to be emotional, not to be moralists, not to be dreamers: to consider our own material interest and nothing but our own material interest: to take stock: to count our advantage. They tell us — some of them in words — some by indirection — that a victory for fascism is in no way different, so far as concerns the Americas at least, from a victory for those opposed to fascism: that if fascism is bloody, Britain is not without blame: that this war, no more than any other war, is a war of evil against good: that there is no issue therefore of good and evil: that we are fools to think so.

They are scornful and cynical voices: and they are wrong. But they are wrong not because they are cynical or because they are coarse or because they lack nobility of mind but for a simpler reason. They are wrong because they are ignorant. They are wrong because they have not understood the American experience and have therefore misjudged the American cause. It is not the American continent we are defending, dear as that continent is to us and beautiful and rich beyond all others.

It is the American idea and the world in which the American idea can live. We are defending that world not because we are idealists or dreamers but because we know — we know at first hand, of our own knowledge — that unless we defend the possibility of a moral order in which the American idea can live we have lost America. Our position is, by the unavoidable necessities of our own defense, a moral position. We must defend the moral order to defend ourselves. And we can defend the moral order to defend ourselves only by accepting for ourselves the moral issue.

It is for this reason that Abraham Lincoln, a great and shadowy figure over three quarters of a century, becomes again with us a living presence. For the greatness of Lincoln consisted precisely in the fact that he reduced the violence and confusion of his time to the essential moral issue and held it there against the cynical and worldly wisdom of the merchants of New England and the brokers of New York and all the rest who argued for expedient self-interest and a realistic view.

The great words of great men have a way of returning from the yellow pages of the manuscripts and the brittle pages of the books and taking breath again and speaking. But rarely have the words of any man three generations dead spoken as Lincoln's words speak now to us. It was on February second in 1863 that Lincoln said to the working men of London: 'The resources, advantages and powers of the American people are very great, and they have consequently succeeded to equally great responsibilities. It seems to have devolved upon them to test whether a government established on the

principle of human freedom can be maintained against
an effort to build one upon the exclusive foundation of
human bondage.' It was in 1863 that these words were
said, but there are men in London now who understand
them — who understand them with a terrible certainty.

But it is not to men in England that the voice of
Lincoln is most urgent and alive. It is to men here:
men in our own country: the cynical, misunderstanding
men who tell us to forget the moral issue — to think of
ourselves — to think of our trade — of our comforts. To
them as to the men who sat in Congress in December,
1862, the voice of Lincoln speaks: 'Fellow citizens, we
cannot escape history. We of this Congress and this
Administration will be remembered in spite of ourselves. No personal significance or insignificance can
spare one or another of us. The fiery trial through
which we pass will light us down in honor or dishonor
to the latest generation. . . . We — even we here — hold
the power and bear the responsibility. . . . We shall
nobly save or meanly lose the last, best hope of earth.'

These words were spoken eighty years ago but the
sound carries. We understand them. We understand
what they say. We understand what they mean also.
We too cannot escape history. We too will be remembered in spite of ourselves. We — even we here — hold
the power and bear the responsibility. We who are
Americans — Canadians and citizens of the United States
alike — will nobly save or meanly lose the last, best hope
of earth. And the fiery trial through which we pass will
light us down — us also — in honor or dishonor.

Our freedom is to choose.

THE PROBLEM OF THE NEW WORLD

★

★

★

★

The Problem of the New World

ADDRESS DELIVERED AT THE
INTER-AMERICAN WRITERS CON-
FERENCE, UNIVERSITY OF PUERTO
RICO, APRIL 18, 1941

IT WAS APPARENT, even before this war began, that there was a new world in being and that the existence of that world created obligations — obligations and difficulties — for those who followed the profession of writer. One cause of our disastrous difficulties was our failure to occupy — imaginatively and understandingly to occupy as only the writer can give us to occupy it — the world in which we lived. Certain scientific discoveries, certain inventions now commonplace, had altered not only the possibilities of the world but its actualities also: not only its dreams but its geography. And our failure to occupy, not only intellectually but imaginatively, not only practically but emotionally, the world thus created, was in large part responsible for the maladjustment and insecurity from which we suffered. It is not physical nature alone which abhors a vacuum nor is it only air and water which flood in to fill the empty space. If men do not occupy for themselves the new continents, the enemies of men will occupy them.

But if it was apparent even before this war that there was a new world in process of creation, it is even more obvious now. There are some, I realize, who still find it possible to believe that the vast struggle of our time is nothing but another 'European war' which we may notice or decline to notice as we please. They are not, however, people whose good judgment — whatever may be said for their good intentions — has impressed their fellow citizens. Aside from this minority and a handful of equally earnest but decidedly less honest people engaged in propagandizing the sword-and-pistol Marxian theory of the imperialist war, the great majority of our contemporaries believe that they have seen what they have seen and heard what they have heard. They believe, that is to say, that fascism is world revolution aimed at the overthrow not only of political systems and economic systems but of social systems as well, and of the entire fabric of moral and cultural values upon which the world as men have known it for many centuries has rested. They differ among themselves only in this — that some of them believe the new order of discipline, authority, and war which fascism proposes to substitute, and has already in many places substituted, for these systems and fabrics is the true shape of the future and must, therefore, be accepted, while others believe the true shape of the future is the very different order of freedom, responsibility, and life which those who hate and fear fascism will be obliged to raise against it as a weapon of their own defense.

But neither those of the first opinion nor those of the second, nor any others who have watched this time with honesty and courage, doubt for a moment that the world we are in process of creating will be a world unlike the world which went before. Those who believe that fascism is the shape of the future can see their future mirrored in a dozen countries and in the faces of the men and women of a hundred once great towns. The rest of us, who believe that democracy, menaced by forces darker, bloodier, and more brutal than those which forced its birth, will of necessity become democracy again and labor and create, can guess our future also. Both worlds are very different from the world we know.

Those who follow the profession of writer seriously and honestly now and in the years which will follow these years will face, therefore, a great obligation and a great difficulty.

The central problem of any art, but, above all, of the art of letters, is the problem of the reduction of experience to form; and a revolutionary change in the structure of experience presents of necessity a revolutionary problem to the artist. The scientist who deciphers experience by abstracting from it absolute quantities can let his absolute quantities stand however violently the reactions of men to each other and the earth may alter; and the philosopher who explains experience by fixing it in abstract terms may pin his abstract terms to the world's skin however the world's skin wrinkles. The artist has no such freedom from change and time. His labor is the labor of translating one form of experience — his life — to another form of experience — his art — and the second must change as the first changes. His labor is to communicate experience in such a way that, by the very act of communication, by the forms of art in which the communication is accomplished, experience itself is re-created — but re-created with coherence and made whole.

As experience alters, therefore, the forms in which experience is re-created and made coherent must alter also. But — and this is the heart of the difficulty — the alteration of forms is never free alteration, pure invention, but always an adaptation of the forms which went before. It is not a new art the artist is contriving but a new use of an art which before had many uses. The artist's problem is to use the formal disciplines which have accomplished the miracle of sensuous translation in other times and with other materials, to accomplish a new miracle of sensuous translation. He brings forward as his tools and implements the inherited devices of his art. And his labor, in a time of profound and unexampled change, is the difficult and arduous labor of compelling the inherited forms of his art to adapt themselves to the necessities of an experience for which they were not devised.

All writers in all countries in which the art of writing continues to be practiced will be committed, in the years which follow the war, to this labor in one form or another, and all will find it difficult. But if it is at all possible in a matter such as this to judge the future by the past — and there is, so far as I know, no other means by which to judge the future — then it is possible, I think, to say that the writers of the Americas will find the difficulties somewhat less than will the writers of other countries. And for this reason: that the history of American letters is precisely the history of a long and difficult apprenticeship in the adaptation of an inherited art of letters to an experience for which that inherited art of letters was in no way devised — an apprenticeship in the adaptation of an art of letters developed in Europe to the experience of life in a country geographically, meteorologically, socially, psychologically, and otherwise unlike the country and the life of Europe.

This, I am well aware, is not the usual description of the literatures of the Americas. The general view, taught in the schools and treated in the scholarly texts, is the view that the literatures of the Americas, certain exceptions duly noted, are principally interesting for two reasons: first, that they are inferior to the European literatures from which they derived; and, second, that their inferiority is to be attributed to the fact that they are colonial. The problem, as the historians have generally seen it, has been the colonial problem, not the problem of the New World. It has been, that is to say, the problem seen from the point of view of Europe and the European tradition, not the problem seen from the point of view of the Americas and the American experience. The weakness of American writers, if you are to believe the books written about them, has been their tendency to the imitation of European writers; and their final enfranchisement will be — or has been — their creation of an American tradition of their own equal in merit to the European tradition from which they derive.

To think at all realistically about the future of American writing or about the work of American writers in the foreseeable future of our world, it is necessary, I think, to re-examine the colonial theory of American art and letters and to inquire how far this theory does really explain what it purports to explain, and how far it leaves out of consideration what no theory dealing with these matters can leave out of consideration. How far, that is to say, are the inadequacies of literature in the Americas explained by explaining merely that literature in the Americas has been colonial? And to what extent is it necessary to have recourse to other theories and explanations to account for the many generations of failure and for the moments of miraculous success?

The colonial theory as I understand it goes something like this: the people of an old world — say, of Europe — have developed certain arts, as for example the arts of cooking and house-building and hide-tanning, and the representation of persons and scenes in colored oils upon canvas, and the composition of accounts and descriptions in words, and the performance of music upon various instruments. These arts and skills are passed along in the usual manner from one generation to another with a minimum of fuss and a variety of consequences but with little or no loss by the way. The new generation learns what it can from the old, does what it must do and what it can do with the means at its disposal, and passes the inheritance on down to those who come after.

This process goes on, interrupted by wars, varied by individual talents, but more or less simply and naturally over long periods of time until, sooner or later, a new land — a new continent or new islands or whatever — is discovered overseas and a migration to those newly discovered countries follows. At which point and without warning, everything is changed. The emigrants — part of the living generation of the old country and co-inheritors, therefore, of its various skills and arts — carry their part of the inheritance out to the new land. They practice there the arts of cooking and house-building, of hide-tanning and oil painting, of stone masonry and music, of the manufacture of textiles and the manufacture of books, which their brothers and their cousins and their contemporaries continue to practice at home.

But the results of their practice are now not at all what they would have been had they remained in the country from which they came. Certain of their arts and skills become more artful, more skillful than they were at home. The emigrants come in time to build better drains. They slaughter better beef. They produce better crops. They manufacture more and better bathtubs. They produce better dentists, better doctors, better engineers, better athletes. But other arts, other skills, deteriorate. And the arts and skills which deteriorate most are always the fine arts, the pure skills — painting, music, and, above all, poetry and letters.

Why poetry and letters should deteriorate among a colonial people, while other inherited arts and skills do not deteriorate, the historians of these matters fail to explain. At least, they fail to explain to those most interested in the problem — the writers and artists of the countries called colonial and so disposed of. American writers wish to learn not that their work is difficult — for they know very well that it is difficult — and not that many American writers in the past have failed — for that, too, is obvious enough — but rather why their difficulties have been so great and why the history of their art in these countries is strewn with so rich and tragical a wreckage. To that sincere and long-asked question the word 'colonial' gives back ambiguous answers.

There is, for one example, the common answer, known to every schoolboy, that the new countries — the colonies — because they are geographically new are also culturally new: because they lack a geographic past, lack also a literary past, and must wait for a past to be accumulated before they can produce a literature of their own. Another is the answer that new countries provide no audiences for the arts and, therefore, can produce no arts. Still another answer is the explanation that the emigrants who go to new countries are not men of the kind who produce poems or music or

paintings; and, therefore, poems and music and paintings must wait for a different kind of man to develop.
All of these statements are accepted as gospel truth by
most of those who talk about the literature of the
Americas. And none of them, I suspect, is even super-
ficially true. I suspect, indeed, that it would be difficult
to think of many generally accepted notions which are
more completely false.

Take first the thesis that the new American countries
failed to produce a great literature throughout their
early history because they were settled by men of adventurous, hardy, and active types who were incapable
of art themselves and incapable of breeding art in their
descendants. The thought apparently is that artists
and particularly writers are bred by other writers — or
at the very least by sedentary persons such as professors,
parsons, dilettantes, and stockbrokers. Nothing could
be farther from the fact. The fact is that writers
descended from other writers, as Mrs. Woolf was from
Thackeray, are the exceptions. Writers rarely breed
good writers and professors almost never. Writers,
painters, and musicians are capable of turning up in
the most unlikely families — and usually do.

Furthermore, it is pure romance to assert that the
Americas were peopled principally by soldiers and bold
adventurous people without nerves, minds, or the
capacity of observation. New countries attract all sorts
and kinds, including many of the principal producers
of literary materials, and the Americas were not exceptions. Soldiers there were, but there were also convicts,
parsons, disappointed revolutionists, politicians out of

favor, younger sons, illegitimate children, persons luck-
less in love, merchants with a nose for bargains, spec-
ulators, fanatics, people who valued liberty, people who
respected their own convictions, and a thousand more
beside — all the sorts, kinds, and species which produce
between them artists, poets, and musicians in any country and at any time.

And as for the soldiers and adventurers themselves —
some of the best writing ever done has come precisely
from such people. I cite, for one, Bernal Diaz del Cas-
tillo; for another, Thucydides.

The same thing is true of the second explanation,
which explains that newly settled countries are countries without background, without culture, without tradition, and, therefore, without the possibility of art and
letters: the explanation which says, 'But America is a
new country: it must wait for time to ripen it.' The
explanation which says, 'There is no American culture
— yet.' As geographical units, the American countries
are 'new,' perhaps — though by no means as new as the
European critics imagine. But as societies considered
in terms of background, of inherited culture, they are
no more new than are the countries of Europe from
which their people came. For their people brought
with them to America the same tradition and the same
culture they left behind them.

The settlers were quite as much the inheritors of the
culture and the tradition of the mother countries as
were the brothers and the first cousins and the first
cousins once removed and the schoolfellows and the
contemporaries they left behind them. If anything,

they were inheritors and heirs more conscious and more zealous than the rest who stayed at home, for the inheritance had to them the added value of all things carried overseas and displayed like a chest of drawers or a box of family silver or a portrait of an ancestor or a leather-bound book in a Boston parlor or a drawing-room in Salta or a hacienda in the Vale of Chile or a sodhouse on the Dakota plains.

It is a matter of common knowledge to all who have traveled in this world that there are no inheritors of tradition or heirs of culture more devoted or more passionate or more opinionated than those who have taken their household goods and their possessions and their memories to the provinces of a new land. Indeed, it is precisely this that the word 'provincial' in its pejorative sense implies. The taste of Boston or of Buenos Aires or of Rio de Janeiro was provincial in the last century because it admired too slavishly and protected too sedulously and possessed too entirely the arts and culture of Britain or of Portugal or of Spain.

The truth is that the people of the newly settled countries possessed the great stream of the inherited tradition down not only to the time of separation but well beyond — and possessed it with a fervor unknown to those who stayed behind. They were snobs of the tradition in a degree far beyond the snobbishness of the mother countries. One has only to consider the unquestioning and pious enthusiasm with which the women of the United States accepted British novelists and British poets, regardless of merit, throughout the nineteenth century and into this.

But if it was not tradition which was lacking in the new countries, or human stock capable of producing writers and artists, neither was it a potential audience. The theory which explains American literary history in terms of the colonial audience is the familiar theory that the people of a newly discovered country are so busy building houses and hewing forests and running surveyors' lines and shooting Indians that they have no time to serve as ears for music or as eyes for poems. It is a plausible theory but it has no basis in fact. It is true, undoubtedly, that the first years of the first settlements in the American countries were laborious and uneasy years. No one in the early years of San Francisco or Plymouth or Deerfield or Jamestown or Vera Cruz or Lima or Rio de Janeiro had much leisure for book-reading — to say nothing of tables, chairs, and candle fat to read by. But in the settlements which endured, this period was always brief — a generation at the most or barely two.

Far from having little time or little need for books, the people of these settlements required books and had time to read them as their descendants never would again. It was in the new settlements, and along the frontier as settlement moved westward, that men had time to read the great books through from end to end, and not once alone but many times — Shakespeare, Camoëns, Cervantes, and the Bible. And it was not only on the frontier that men in the United States had time and appetite for reading. Jefferson's library, the purchase of which was the true founding of the Library of Congress, was not the only great library in Virginia, nor was Virginia the only state of the United States to possess magnificent collections of great works. Neither in the United States nor elsewhere in the Americas was there any lack of men with appetites for books and means to possess them.

The truth, in other words, is that the theory of American letters which explains the inadequacies of American literature over many generations, and even centuries, on the ground that the American countries were colonial countries is considerably less than adequate. For one thing, it does not explain what it purports to explain. For another, it is mischievous. The young American writer who thinks of American letters as the critics have taught him to think of American letters, begins very shortly to think of his own work in the same terms: begins, that is, to tell himself that his task is to produce not a poem or a novel or a play but 'literature' — 'literature' equal if possible to the literature of Europe, but in any case 'literature.'

A very considerable part of the self-consciousness which afflicted American writing a generation ago, and even less, was the direct and natural consequence of this attitude. The preoccupation with 'literature,' the preoccupation with The Tradition, which was so familiar a decade or so ago, was an American contribution to the art of letters and could have been nothing else. Only Americans bred in the colonial theory of American letters could have thought of the art of writing as the art of adding to the tradition of English literature. To less self-conscious men the purpose of the art of writing is writing; and the tradition is a means which one employs if one can — a means which becomes an end only when the work is finished and the tradition accepts it or rejects it as history determines.

But the chief indictment of the colonial theory of American letters is graver than this. The chief indictment of the colonial theory is that it leaves out of account the true reason, the honorable reason, for the many and repeated failures of the art of letters in these countries, and neglects, therefore, the considerations upon which a true understanding of the American literatures or of their future may be based. The colonial theory is the theory of a new literature as it appears to those who continue to occupy, either physically or psychologically, the countries from which the colonists went out. But the problem with which the serious writers of the Americas have wrestled for centuries is not the problem of the emulation of Old-World writers, nor the self-conscious attempt to escape from emulation into a new American tradition.

The problem with which the writers of the Americas have struggled has been the problem of the New World: the problem of a new literature as it looks to those who have brought the older culture with them to conditions and surroundings in which the forms of the older culture are foreign, inappropriate, and strange. The colonial problem is a problem imposed by emigration from a known country; the problem of the New World is a problem imposed by the occupation of a new. To European critics it is only important that the ancestors of American writers went *from* Spain or Portugal or England or the continent of Europe. To American

writers, it is infinitely more important that their ancestors — or they themselves — came *to* America.

The difference is real. But it is not merely geographical. It involves also a difference — an ancient and
frequently embittered difference — between the poet's
concept of the art of letters and the critic's: between
the concept which sees the art of letters as the art of
creating *this* poem, *this* novel, *this* play, and the concept which sees it as a great number of poems, plays,
and novels already written and now to be arranged together in a certain order, or a certain organism, called
the literature or the tradition of the tongue. To the
critic, feeling backward down his coral reef from the
surface-present to the deep and crumbling rubble far
below, the labor of the creation of a single coral cell or
branch of cells has small importance. To the poet it
has the supreme importance of an act unique and single
in the world. To the critic the art of letters is literature, and literature is in the past — an old existing
country which needs but roads and road maps to be
known. To the poet the art of letters is an art, and art
is in the present — a process frequently repeated and
never finally performed: the process of reducing to a
form at once sensuous and intelligible the fragmentary,
reluctant, and inarticulate experience of men upon this
earth — the process, that is to say, the one known process, by which men present to themselves an image of
their lives and so possess them. The art of letters to the
poet is the mirror of time — the only mirror men have
ever found of time.

The problem of the New World, then, is a poet's

problem, not a critic's. It is the problem faced by those
to whom the practice of the art of letters is the practice
of the art by which experience is reduced to form —
and who practice that art in a world in which the experience of men is new and unaccustomed — and the
forms are old. It is, in other words, *the* poet's problem
carried to the farthest point of difficulty. The labor of
the poet is difficult in any country and at any time. But
in a new country — in a continent in which the experience of men alters but the forms of art are old — it is
a labor of which the difficulty is almost immeasurable.
The raw material, the stubborn facts, of an experience
never before resolved into art must be resolved: the
raw material of geography, climate, the nervous reactions of men, their tricks and gestures, what they do
here that they have not done elsewhere and what they
do not do, how they get on with the new sun and the
new rain and the animals, how they are with each
other and how not, how they sleep and what images
come to their sleep. But this is not the whole difficulty. It is not even the principal difficulty. The principal difficulty is that this experience must be communicated in forms of art never intended for its communication — forms of art unrelated to the experience on
which they move.

In an old country, an ancient civilization like that of
China in its great period, or a less ancient but, none
the less, habitual civilization like that of England in
the seventeenth century — a society which continues
from generation to generation in surroundings more or
less unchanged — in such a country, the relation be-

tween the forms of art and the pattern of experience is
easy and familiar: so easy and so familiar that the two
are tangled into one and cannot be untangled. The
references are immediate and immediately understood,
the allusions are a second speech and equally intelligible, the responses of emotion are as natural and certain as echoes from an old-built wall.

But in a new country, and, above all, in a new country in which everything is different — seasons, geography, and men — there is no such familiar and habitual
relation between art and lives. There is, on the contrary, a lack of relation which is more than a mere absence of that quality: which becomes instead a positive
obstacle, an intrusive discord. The inherited forms of
art carried to the new country by settlers and there em-
ployed are not only not forms developed in the new
country for the communication of its experience but,
instead, forms developed in a different country for the
communication of a different experience. They are,
therefore and necessarily, forms which carry with them
the tone, the color, the remembrance of the old experience. The principal reason why the labor of the poet
in a new country is difficult is that this tone, this color,
bred into the forms of his art, twisted into the sounds
and meanings of his words, impossible therefore to
avoid or evade, falsifies and discolors and distorts the
image of the world he lives in, out of which he writes.

It is this fact, a fact well known to every sensitive
writer of this hemisphere whether he writes in English
or in Spanish or in Portuguese, which defines the true
American problem in the art of letters. To represent

by the use of a medium which carries in the fiber of its structure reflections and refractions of an altogether different experience — to represent by such a medium the experience of a new and altered world — is the labor to which the writers of the Americas have been committed from the beginning of their history. It, and not the colonial problem, not the problem defined by European critics, not the problem described by American writers in violent revolt against their work, their fellow workers, and themselves, is the problem common to us all.

The entire history of letters in this continent demonstrates that fact. Early writers in all our countries have been blamed by later critics because they wrote of America as though it lay in the valley of the Tagus or the yellow hills of Navarre or the sheep pastures of Devon. Nature, the critics complained, came to Anne Bradstreet, the seventeenth-century New England poetess, not directly but 'as something which had to be translated into the regular rhythm and rhetorical exaggerations of the English school of the time.' But it was not Anne Bradstreet or her contemporaries of the other Americas who were at fault. Nor are later writers chargeable with moral turpitude and artistic dishonesty because they continued for two hundred years and still sometimes continue to write of American life in books and poems which could have been written equally well by Europeans who had never crossed the Atlantic.

The literary suicides of the Americas — the many Americans who destroyed themselves as American

writers by one means or another — testify not to the indifference of the writers of these countries but to the
difficulty of their task. These suicides — for suicides
they are — are commonplaces in our literary history
both north and south. Some men of talent, unable to
compel the art to serve their purposes, resigned the
effort altogether. Some, although they continued to
write, gave up the attempt to write as men living in
their own time and in the Americas, and wrote instead
and deliberately as though they had lived a hundred
years before and in a different country. Others again
emigrated physically, as these last emigrated psychologically, returning from the New World to the Old and
settling again in the surroundings and the society to
which the forms they had inherited belonged. Still
others escaped in an opposite direction, emigrating not
from the new experience but from the tradition of the
art, destroying themselves in anarchy and ignorance.
Even the best, the most courageous and most skillful,
were incapable over many generations of mastering the
American experience *and* communicating it in forms
derived from the traditions of the art. It was not until
Mark Twain that writers of the United States forced
their art to serve them as Americans, and it was not
until the present generation — the generation of Hemingway and Dos Passos and Faulkner — that an American novel was written which could at once move easily
in the great tradition of English letters and at the same
time occupy and master the American experience of
living men.

It would be untrue and unwise beside to say, in con-

clusion of this matter, that American writers have
solved for themselves the problem with which they have
struggled for so long. Latin American poetry is as fine
as any poetry now written, and the novel in the United
States has surpassed the British novel with which it was
so long and so unfavorably compared; but it would be
presumptuous notwithstanding to pretend that the
American experience and the old inherited forms of the
art of letters have now at last been matched. Nevertheless, if it is true as I believe it to be true that the labor
of letters in our own time and in the time beyond us is
the labor imposed upon us by a new and undiscovered
world, then the work done and the failures suffered in
these continents will have their use. For in that labor
the writers of the four Americas have served a long apprenticeship and gained some knowledge.

There are those I know who doubt that writers have
played or can play an effective part in the histories of
their peoples. There are, among others, the contemporary determinists who inform us that the proper rôle
of the writer is merely to give words to a popular will
which would have existed in any case without him — a
will driven by economic and historic forces beyond the
power of any man to direct or control. But though the
opinion is very broadly held, I doubt that it has reason.
I doubt that fatalism is a truer formula since Marx
than it was before, or that it is any more admirable to
surrender the will of men to the will of fate under a
scientific name than under a mythological. But whether
it is true or not that writers should be the followers of
human destiny rather than the instigators of human

purpose, one thing is clear and certain: that no pur-
posed human action is conceivable without an image of
the world which is coherent and distinguishable, and
that the creation of such an image of the world, recog-
nizable to the emotions as well as to the mind, is the
work of which the artist moving in the forms and words
of art is capable.

Without such an image of the world and of their
lives, men inevitably fall into such a surrender of the
will, such a mute reliance upon mechanistic forces, as
our time, and the generation particularly to which I
belong, has made. It is because the world of our time
seems to most of those who live in it to have lost its
coherence and its meaning that the economic fatalities
of the communists, and the wave-like and inevitable
futures of the fascists, have had such power in men's
minds. In a shadowy and chaotic world where nothing
has reality and all the enemies are shadows, surrender
to the mechanistic fates, the predetermined futures, becomes the only sure escape for frightened men. Those
of us, therefore, who do not love the mechanistic fates
or the predetermined futures will continue to believe
that the writers of our own time and of the time beyond us must undertake to reduce to sunlight and recognition the shadowy chaos of our world, providing us,
in place of the unopposable and terrifying shadows,
an understandable experience of life with which the
will of men can deal. For it is only by seeing their
experience of the world for what it is — however terrible — that men can act upon it.

I have no wish to prophesy and no authority to read

the future. But it seems to me possible, notwithstanding, that the writers of the four Americas — writers to whom the problem of the New World is a known and a familiar problem — may perhaps undertake this labor more willingly, and accomplish it with greater courage, than other writers will in other countries. It seems to me conceivable, in other words, that the long apprenticeship of the Americans, the centuries of labor and the fierce defeats, may perhaps end now in such a literature — so strong, so boldly knowing, so perfect to its time — that others who come after us will say the labor was the prologue to a noble art, and all the pain worth bearing.

TO THE CLASS OF 1941

★

★

★

★

To the Class of 1941

COMMENCEMENT ADDRESS DELIVERED
AT UNION COLLEGE, JUNE 9, 1941

COLLEGE CLASSES ARE REMEMBERED through the brief
periods of college history for one characteristic or
another — the largest or the brightest or the tallest or
the wildest or the luckiest or whatever. Your class, not
here only but throughout the United States, will be
remembered as the most talked-at class since the first
divinity student said good-bye to the last cow in the
Harvard cow yard and headed west to Watertown to
convert the Indians. Compared with any college class
of recent history — compared with my own class which
graduated into the world of 1915 — compared even with
the class of 1917 which heard the echoing oratory of

actual war — you are the most consistent objects of
other people's talk of which there is any record. I have
no doubt but that you are thoroughly sick by now of
the whole business — the talk, the talkers, and even of
yourselves as the objects of talk. A satisfactory commencement to most of you would be a commencement
without words at all and certainly without words directed at the opinions, orthodox or otherwise, of the
graduating class.

You will not have, I am afraid, a satisfactory commencement. And for a reason which relates not to the
motives of those who have been invited to speak to you
but to very different considerations. Neither you nor
they nor anyone else can avoid the discussions of
opinion at this moment in the history of the world because, at this moment in history, opinion is of greater
importance than anything else of which men can think
or speak. And neither you nor they can avoid the dis-
cussion of your opinions because, of all opinions of
which men can think or speak, yours are most immediately significant. The debate which has been going
forward over the past twelve months between members
of your generation and members of mine is not a frivolous debate, nor is the attempt by one group or
another to define or to modify your views a gratuitous
and impertinent interference with matters private to
yourselves. Whether the contestants realize it or not,
they are engaged in a struggle as important to the outcome of this war as any other — perhaps more important. For in a sense which is not at all figurative or
poetic you are the principal battleground of this war —

you and a great many million others, but first, and
most directly, you — the young men and young women
of every country, and particularly of this.

There are some among you who, thinking of 1914
and of 1860 and of other years, claim special consideration for your opinions because you will do the fighting
in this war if there is fighting to be done. Young men
will not fight this war any more than old men and
women and children will fight it: the experience of
England would seem to show that they may even fight
it less. But the opinions, the beliefs of young men and
young women have nevertheless an importance in this
war which neither they nor we may always realize. We
speak most frequently in geographic terms when we
speak of the war — and in geographic terms of a vast-
ness which excites us. For us there are no battles of
Agincourt or Waterloo or Manassas; engagements
fought on a single plain or on a hillside or in the fields
about a town or on a sloping ridge. For us the battles
are battles of France, battles of Britain, battles of the
Atlantic. But even these enormous titles of geography
and war are smaller than the truth. For the true battleground is not an extent of land at all or even an
ocean or a sea. It is larger still. It is the minds of
young men.

It is the minds of young men not in poetic metaphor
but in the most precise and literal truth. The Nazis
may win all the battles of geography — they may defeat
all their enemies and subdue the continent of Europe
as they have now subdued the greater part of that continent, they may win the battle of Africa, the battle of

Asia, even the battle of the Atlantic, but they will not
have *won* the war, however thoroughly the peoples of
England and all other peoples who have courage to
oppose them will have *lost* the war — they will not have
won the war unless and until they have persuaded the
minds of millions of human beings to accept the kind
of world they propose to create.

They know this well enough. Their first effort in
every country they have conquered has been to win the
minds of the young men and the young women to their
cause — to persuade the young men and the young
women of Denmark and Norway and Holland and Belgium and France that democracy is corrupt, fat, deca-
dent, and dying: that only discipline and blind obedience to the Nazi will can give the young men jobs again
and the young women marriage and children. You cannot combine millions of human beings in a going and
effective economic system coordinated for industrial
production on the modern scale by billeting troops in
their towns or by lodging secret police in their homes
or even by torturing those who resist and shooting their
mothers. To *win* the war as the Nazis mean to win it
is not merely to destroy the cities of those who fight
back and to cripple their children with bombs and to
liquidate their writers and their teachers in the cellars
of warehouses and to send their scientists and their
preachers to rot behind barbed wire. To win the war
as the Nazis mean to win it is to win the minds of whole
populations of human beings to affirmative cooperation
in a 'New Order' of which the fascist slogan is the perfect description: 'Believe, obey, fight.' The one battle,

therefore, which the Nazis and their satellites must win
is the battle for belief.

But the same necessity compels those also who are
determined to resist the establishment of such a system:
who are determined to resist the Nazification of the
world. They too must win the battle of men's minds.
They must first of all bring millions of men to desire to
resist a danger which is not real to most of them until
it can no longer be resisted — men who hate war as all
sane and serious human beings hate war; men who
have, or think they have, nothing of their own to fight
for; men who wish only to be left alone, to be passed
by, to be forgotten. They must bring millions of such
men to *see* the things they look at; to listen to the
sounds they hear, to understand that these horrors of
which they read, of which they speak, are actual things,
things which have actually happened and are now happening and will continue to happen unless they are
stopped. They must bring millions of such men to understand with the final shock of personal understanding
that in this war it is not possible for any man, no matter how anonymous, no matter how indifferent, no matter how small, to be passed by, to be left alone; that
this is not that kind of war; that the outcome of this
war will affect every man, whatever his wishes, that
'there are none neutral in this war'; that 'no personal
significance or insignificance will spare one or another
of us.'

But even this necessity is only the beginning of the
necessities which drive those men and women who understand what Naziism is and who propose to resist it

and to persuade others to resist it while they still can.
They must not only win the beginning of that battle:
they must not only persuade men who are not yet slaves
to resist slavery: but they also — they as much as the
Nazis — must win the remainder of the fight. They
too must persuade men's minds to accept — and not
only to accept but to affirm, as a man affirms a cause in
which he believes and has faith — they too must persuade men's minds to accept an organization of life.
They must bring men to believe, or to believe again,
in the possibility of freedom.

There are two reasons why they must persuade men's
minds of this: first, they, no more than the Nazis, will
have *won* the war if they do no more than destroy the
Nazi weapons and break the power of their dictators.
To do that much is to win a tremendous victory and
yet to win nothing, for Naziism is not Hitler but an evil
with a long and bloody past, a snake with innumerable
lives and as many heads as there are swords to strike
them off. That is the first reason. The second is this:
that unless the partisans of freedom persuade men's
minds to accept as their own and to declare as their
cause the cause of freedom, they will not even win the
fruitless, the negative preliminary victory against armies
and machines. For unless they can persuade men's
minds of this, they will oppose to the disciplined and
propagandized and indoctrinated armies of the fascists
— soldiers brought up and educated to believe the fascist lie and to believe it not only with their lips but
with their souls — they will then oppose to such an
army an army altogether lacking in any affirmative be-

lief, an army prepared only to resist and hence an army more than half defeated from the start.

This then is the real battle of this war — the battle fought upon that darkling plain of the human spirit of which Arnold wrote — the battle of which you and millions like you are the field. It is a battle fought not with bombs or with guns or ships, although bombs and guns and ships play their real and terrible part. It is a battle fought with words: words which also are realities and can be terrible. It is a decisive battle upon the outcome of which the future of the world does truly depend. And it is a battle from which no man or woman of your generation or mine or any other can abstain or stand apart.

But it is not only because this battle must be fought that your elders have busied themselves so long and so insistently with your opinions. There is another reason also — a reason which your elders do not perhaps admit to themselves or altogether realize but which is nevertheless a continuing presence in their minds. The reason is that this battle is not only critical but, for the partisans of freedom, the fighters against fascism, desperate — as desperate as the battle of machines and men has thus far proved to be in Europe. For in this battle as in that, those to whom we are opposed have the advantage of weapons and position. In words as in planes and tanks the destroyers of liberty, the enemies of freedom, have an initial superiority which will not easily be overcome. And this superiority is a superiority for which, even more than their superiority in tanks and planes, we ourselves must take responsibility. For it is

a superiority we have helped create, not, as is the case
of physical weapons, by negligence and inaction, but by
action and by positive default. We, partisans of freedom and believers in the government of the people by
themselves, have not only deprived ourselves of a power
of words which should have been ours: we have placed
in the hands of those who would destroy us the weapons
by which they can effectively attack. We have established upon the field of opinion — upon the field specifically of the opinion of men and women of the generation to which you belong — weapons and positions
which can be used only by our enemies and not ourselves — weapons and positions which they have already
seized and turned against us.

Words as weapons are of two kinds in such a war as
this. A bomb is a bomb no matter who drops it or on
whom — the English on the Nazis or the Nazis on the
English: it falls, it explodes, it kills regardless of the
sender and regardless of the target. But words, in this
war, are not alike. The words which the Nazis can use
as weapons are not the words we can use, nor are the
words which can be weapons for us weapons for them.
The enemies of freedom whose only cause is negation
and denial — government by the secret police and the
cellar murder — can use words as weapons only to destroy: to destroy belief in human worth, human dignity, human capacity for action: to destroy all human
hope of human and voluntary solution of the problems
of our lives: to destroy all confidence in human will but
the one will imposed by the ruler and perfected in the
State. The partisans of freedom, on the other hand,

whose only cause is freedom and responsibility of men and mind, must use the words of affirmation and of faith. Only those words are weapons in their hands which can create and re-create the self-respect of men, their confidence of men in their own worth and their own power, their belief in themselves and in the life they can create together.

The weapons of the Nazis — the weapons they use with the populations they have subdued by force of arms and must convince to conquer — the weapons they use with the populations of more distant countries whom they wish to paralyze with doubt and fear until their own time comes — their weapons are therefore what we know: the words powerful in destruction, powerful in negation, powerful in doubt. They are the words which define democracy in such a way as to destroy all faith in democracy; the words which shake belief in liberty, in freedom, in free-will, in self-government; which debunk, discredit: the words, in short, which have for purpose to drive their listeners, disillusioned and disgusted with themselves and every man, into the iron arms of discipline and obedience and slavery, not out of love of discipline and slavery, but out of disillusion and contempt of other orders of the world.

And for the same reason the weapons of those who oppose fascism and who would bring against it the affirmative passion for freedom in a free man's world by which alone fascism can be defeated, are the affirmative, the candid and believing words, which say that men have dignity, that men have value, that all men are created free and equal, that the earth, as Jefferson said again, belongs to the living generation. Their words are the words used not to deny but to affirm, not to obscure but to clarify, not to destroy credit but to create credit, not to corrupt belief but to create belief. They are the words of the great hopes, the recurring dreams, the indestructible declarations.

Where the Nazis aim by their use of words at doubt, discredit, and dissension, those who oppose the Nazis aim by the same means at faith and loyalty and common agreement. Where the Nazis intend by their use of words to infect their hearers with such cynicism as to human nature, such disgust with popular government, such hopelessness of any democratic solution, that men will turn, each man away from all other men, toward a dictator, a man of force, who will impose order upon all the rest and compel their obedience, those who oppose fascism intend by their use of words to create such a belief in human decency, such faith in the power of the people to govern themselves, such hope of the kind of world a free people can create for itself, that men will turn, not away from each other, but toward each other — so that men will accept their responsibilities as co-governors of themselves rather than surrendering those responsibilities to a common master who will rule them all.

That the second use of words as weapons in this war is more difficult than the first goes without saying. Creation is always more difficult than destruction, and never more so than when the material of creation or destruction is confidence and belief. But in the present struggle of discredit against credit, of human despair against human hope, the uses of words to destroy have an added advantage in this country and with the generation to which you belong. It is an advantage we have not only permitted them to gain but which we have ourselves created for them. And it is because this advantage exists, and because it is an advantage great enough perhaps to turn the war against us, that we speak as we do, with such insistence and such passion — even with such personal bitterness — of the issue of belief. The advantage is this: that the generation to which you belong is already, by education and by experience, far more ready to respond to the use of language to discredit and disillusion and destroy than to the use of language to declare and to affirm.

Whether they so realize or not, the bitterness with which your elders have sometimes spoken of your opinions and beliefs is a bitterness which comes from their sense of their own responsibility and blame. One may shift the blame as one pleases but it returns always to our heads. Whether the verbal defensiveness and skepticism of your generation is to be attributed to the success of the so-called scientific vocabulary in your teaching, or to the inflation and distortion of language in the commercial appeals of industry and business, or to the abuse of language in the declarations of public men, or to the cult of irony — the language of defeat and self-defense — in the literature of the twenties and the thirties, or more realistically to the discrepancy between the world as it appears in the textbooks and the newspapers and the conversations of substantial persons, and the world as it looks from a train window or across the desk of an employment office where there is no employment — however one defines the cause, the responsibility belongs to us. And it is not a responsibility easy to bear.

A great part of the American people — the younger part particularly, and, of that younger part, the more highly educated, the more intelligent — has developed over the past decade and a half a suspicion of words, a doubt of the validity of all verbal affirmations, an automatic distrust of declarations of belief, an equally automatic distrust of eloquence, of emotion, a fear of being moved, or being persuaded, of being brought to affirm and to declare, which becomes, in its extreme forms, a kind of reverse gullibility — a gullibility which accepts without question, and in every case, the discreditable explanation while doubting in every case with equal simple-mindedness the creditable appearance — a simple-minded gullibility which assumes as a matter of course that all the gold is brick, that all the complexions are false, that all the virtues are hypocrisies, that there is a low-down to everything, and that the only wisdom is to be wise not as the great were wise but as the wise-crack is 'wise' — as the tough are 'wise' around the drugstore corner.

It is the gullibility which finds readers for the side-slip publications of our time which purport to tell the 'inside story,' the 'actual facts'— usually with a pair of scissors and a pot of paste to tell them with. It is the gullibility which leads young men and young women, sophisticated and duly suspicious in all other matters, to

accept without question the inside story, the actual
facts, as they are presented by the country's least objective journalists, in the official publications of private
political parties and other claques and cliques which
have never claimed an interest in the truth — nor
earned the right to claim it.

The responsibility for all this is our responsibility,
but there is another responsibility which is yours: We
cannot ask you to believe, by an effort of will, in the
possibility of an organization of the world for freedom
through the means of freedom. We cannot ask you to
will to believe any more than you can ask us, as some of
you have asked us, to do your believing for you. But
what we can ask you to do is to face the question of
belief as fairly as the world we have made and the education we have given you will let you: to be as suspicious of suspicion as you are of affirmation; to be no
more afraid to confess belief than you are to admit
doubt; to be as trustful of passion and emotion as of
skepticism and emotional impotence — even when it
describes itself as scientific doubt.

Maintain if you will the attitude of the objective
searcher after truth in which you have been trained,
but refuse to let that attitude betray you into credulous
acceptance of all doubters. Put us both on trial for our
truth and for our lives — we who have failed to create a
true democracy in this country or in the world and
these others who now offer you obedience and discipline
instead; we who have created for you a society, an economic order, which neither you nor we can take much
pride in, and these others who would give you in its

place a different order made by the police. Put us both on trial and choose between us, but remember, as you choose, the choice you make is for yourselves. Remember that, although this battle for men's minds is fought upon the field of your opinions, you will be its winners or its losers also; and the choice is yours.

What we can demand of you, and what you can demand with even greater authority of yourselves, is that you put off the irresponsibility you have learned from us, the irresponsibility of those who wear suspicion as an armor and doubt as a disguise — those to whom the scientist's detachment is a trick by which the life-and-death commitments of belief may be avoided — those who evade their time by hiding in the cotton wool of doubt and skepticism and refusal. What you can demand with honor of yourselves is this: that you accept the issue history has forced upon you and that you come to your decision on that issue not by default and not by refusal, but in the full responsible determination to decide your future for yourselves. More than that, no man, neither you nor we, can ask.

PROPHETS OF DISASTER

*

*

*

*

Prophets of Disaster

COMMENCEMENT ADDRESS DELIV-
ERED AT THE UNIVERSITY OF
PENNSYLVANIA, JUNE 11, 1941

IT IS THE CUSTOM of this country to offer up a certain quantity of words on the graduation from college of each annual generation of young men. It was the custom of other countries to offer up on such occasions a certain quantity of bull's blood. In both cases, it was the sacrificial act and not the thing sacrificed which counted. With the ancients the blood itself was not valued. The earth took it. The practice is the same with us. We prefer, perhaps unwisely, the gullets of men to the gullets of cattle and — unwisely perhaps again — we do not cut them. But with us, as with those

others, it is the full luxurious flow which is counted as
auspicious. No one intends to gather up the words and
preserve them for the future guidance of his life.

I mention this not to complain of it but to indicate
that I understand my rôle and accept it. I accept, that
is to say, the unexpressed stipulation that I am not to
communicate a message of meaning and significance, or
deliver to you in useful and memorable form the
truths my generation knows which your generation does
not know. It is not difficult to accept. What a man
knows at fifty that he did not know at twenty is, for the
most part, incommunicable — which is, perhaps, why
no adequate system of education has ever yet been devised. The 'laws,' the aphorisms, the generalizations,
the universal truths, the parables and the old saws — all
the observations about life which can be communicated
readily in handy verbal packages — are as well known
to a man at twenty as at fifty: he has been told them all,
he has read them all, and he has probably repeated them
all before he graduates from college.

What he knows at fifty that he did not know at
twenty is little more than this: that the things he was
told were true at twenty and the things he said were
true at twenty are, for the most part, *really* true — but
true with a brutal and inescapable truthfulness and
consequence and meaning which would have shocked
him had he guessed at it thirty years before. This
knowledge is of all forms of knowledge the least com-
municable because it is a knowledge not of formulas or
forms of words but of people, places, actions — a
knowledge never gained by words but by touch, sight,

delays, victories, sleeplessness, shame, love — briefly by experience of this earth and of oneself and other men.

How difficult it is to communicate you may see for yourselves by observing carefully the efforts of the greatest poets to communicate it — for this labor is the last and most difficult of all the labors of poetry. Between a poem of Yeats which says, in the twentieth year of his life, that women are beautiful, and a poem of Yeats which speaks thirty years afterward of the beauty of women, there is a difference which, to a young man and to any woman, is no difference at all, but to a man in middle life immeasurable.

So that it is not a hindrance but, on the contrary, a considerable help to accept the custom of these ceremonies. I willingly agree to burden you with no secrets and to charge you with no knowledge private to your elders. But though I am not myself to communicate messages from beyond your fortieth year or to bring you words in a sealed bottle from voyages which preceded your voyage — stuffed birds from remote islands or photographs of the customs of the inhabitants — there is, nevertheless, one thing I am at liberty to do; one thing which, perhaps, I have a certain obligation to do. I am at liberty to warn you against certain members of my generation who do not accept for themselves the restrictions you impose upon me here but openly undertake, not only in rooms privately but in public addresses and even in books to communicate what cannot be communicated and to convey what has no conveyance.

That there are such members of my generation is not

unknown to you. The social historians whose duty it is to record interesting phenomena have thus far failed to record the fact that my generation has produced prophets, but you have not failed to notice it. Too many of the prophecies have been aimed at you. You have had occasion to observe that there are members of my generation who are familiar with the shape of the future and who are willing to share their familiarity with others. You have heard voices which declare that the violence and brutality and obscurantism which you see sweeping over the world are the present shape of the future and should be welcomed for that reason. You have heard still other voices intoning the news that there is nothing to do about this violence and this obscurantism but let it sweep over you; that if you attempt to defend your kind of world against it you will inevitably lose your kind of world. You have had other advisers also — those who speak in the rôle of the old soldiers — plucking your sleeves and telling you they were tricked into the last war by talk of democracy; telling you the talk of democracy is always talk to trick a man; telling you that you also, if you listen, if you weigh the democratic risk, will be tricked and made fools of. You have heard the professors prophesying that the violence of this time will take its course as the violence of the French Revolution took its course and that nothing you can do or fail to do will change the outcome — the military strategists prophesying that those who oppose this violence will inevitably fall regardless of any aid of ours, and that we ourselves will inevitably suffer humiliation and defeat if we attempt to lift a hand to help them.

But though you are aware of the presence and of the prophecies of these people, you have not, I believe, considered with attention what they are or why they speak as they do, and it is for this reason that I feel compelled to warn you.

Briefly, there are three observations to be made about these prophecies. Each relates to the others and all three to the credibility of the prophetic words. They are not observations which are frequently brought to mind, at least in public discussions of these matters.

The first is this: that these prophecies *are* prophecies. Prophets have been infrequent in recent centuries and the sudden appearance of numbers of them in the time in which we live, foretelling the future to the young and informing them of the disasters which will inevitably follow certain actions, is a curious phenomenon.

The second observation is the observation that all these prophecies are prophecies of defeat, prophecies of negation, prophecies not of the things which men can do but of the things which men cannot do. This too is unusual. Prophets have prophesied disaster before this, but rarely as consistently or in such numbers, and rarely in terms of impotence and failure so complete.

The third observation is less dramatic but no less interesting for that. It is the observation that these prophetic voices are not, as was the case in antiquity, the voices of old men but of men and women in middle life — men and women of the generation which knew in its childhood or its youth the other war and which came to consciousness of the world and of itself in the years between. It was not common in any

ancient people that men and women in the full strength
of their middle years prophesied publicly and always of
disaster and defeat.

These three observations have significance because
they bear upon the question any curious listener to
these words will wish to ask himself: Why do these
men and women prophesy and why, if they must fore-
tell the future to us, do they tell it in these terms? Is it
because they possess a knowledge of the future not
possessed by other men or is there a different reason?
And if there is a different reason is it a reason which
has to do with the thing the speakers have in common
— their age — their common generation?

The answer, I think, is not too difficult. Prophets
appear only among those who know, or who think they
know, that the pattern of life is determined beforehand
and who know, or who think they know, that they are
privy to its determination. The generation to which I
belong believes, as you who have read its books are
aware, in a predetermined pattern of life. It is our conviction, explicitly stated in our histories, our political
commentaries, and our studies in economics, implicitly
stated in our novels and our poetry, that the pattern of
life is determined by Economic Law or Historical Necessity or Psychological Compulsion and that we are, or by
taking thought can make ourselves, privy to these Laws
and these Necessities. We not only believe in a predetermined pattern of life, which is to say, in Fate: we believe in it to a degree unknown in western civilization
for centuries. It is probable therefore that it is not because they have been touched by a god's breath or be-

cause they have beheld visions at night but for a simpler reason that these prophets prophesy: they prophesy because they belong to a generation which, whether it so admits or not, believes, and has believed for years, in Fate and because, therefore, prophecy is natural to them.

Why these prophets prophesy in the language of impotence and defeat is however a more complicated question and one which requires for its understanding a more extended consideration of the relation between my generation and the notion of fate. The fact that men of a given time believe in a predetermined pattern of life does not necessarily mean that they are fatalists or that their prophecies must take fatalistic form. The Greeks, for example, were believers in fate and producers of prophecies but not of prophecies like these. For the Greeks conceived of fate not as a predetermined pattern controlling the whole of life and controlling therefore the will and acts of men but as a divine intervention capable of cutting across the acts of men at unexpected moments.

Fate, to the Greeks, was a force to be reckoned with, a force to be respected, even a force to be feared. But fate was never an inevitable pattern to which history and all men's hopes must be resigned. Odysseus, most Greek of all Greek heroes, outwitted the implacable will where he could, and it is the chorus of Sophocles in the Antigone which says, 'Many wonders there are but nothing more wonderful than man.' A man among the Greeks was not relieved of the necessity of choice or of the responsibility for choosing because an unalter-

able will had already chosen in his stead. Nor was it
either honorable or admirable for a man among the
Greeks to accept and to admit that he accepted the
domination of his world by forces beyond his power to
control, fitting his life to their patterns and living at
their will. The fates were not an inevitable force, but
a three-named god, and with a god, with God's help, a
man could struggle, surrendering only when he had no
choice but to surrender. To the Greeks, in short, man
was capable of the mastery of the greater part of a
human and sunlit world and only the shadowy edges,
the dark depths of unforeseeable mischance, were left to
the inscrutable and fatal will. Men could be destroyed
and were often destroyed by inconceivable disaster, but
they were capable also of compelling the human world
— and sometimes the non-human. They were capable
of victories against odds, achievements in the face of im-
probabilities — Thermopylae, Salamis.

Our view of fate — the view entertained by men of
my generation — differs, however, in every sense from
the Greek. It differs even in the manner in which it
was formed. The Greeks learned the will of fate by
opposing to it their own wills, determining for themselves, by their own defeats, by their own experience,
what limits are placed upon the freedom of men to act
and at what point it is seemly and proper for a man to
bend his will to that other will. Our generation ascer-
tained the will of fate not by opposing it, not even by
yielding to it when we met it, but by searching it out in
order that we might yield to it and by yielding then our
will and our responsibilities. And the fate which we

searched out — the fate of universal economic laws and universal historical necessities — was a fate which accounted not only for the margins of our lives, the twilight of inexplicable event, but for our lives themselves and the entire world in which we lived.

The Greeks discovered fate across their paths. We fled to fate to escape a world which had grown too large for us, a world too complicated to understand, too huge to rule. The innovations of our period — the plane, the radio, the automobile — did not, as clumsy speakers sometimes say, *contract* our world. On the contrary, they extended our world, or extended at least our experience of our world, until the physical hearing, the physical sight, and almost the physical presence of an individual man were pushed out to cover an area of which previously he could have had no physical and personal knowledge. This physical extension of a single man's experience moreover was accompanied by no increased extension of his competence to deal with his experience. No innovation in the physical sciences, and no triumph of education equipped him to deal either with the larger world he saw and heard himself or with the tangled and complicated world of tangled and complicated social and economic relations which lay beyond his personal experience and behind it.

We became, all of us, huge and gawky shadows of ourselves such as a level autumn sun throws out across a meadow and a hill to stumble and gesticulate and fade. We seemed suddenly huge and we touched the earth more broadly, but we ourselves were still no larger than we ever were. We realized our smallness, our inadequacy. The thought frightened us, and we accepted willingly and even eagerly the image of a world directed by historical necessity and economic law. We accepted it, not as the Greeks accepted the existence of the fates — a power to be reckoned with, a force to be evaded or avoided as long as evasion was possible — but as the creatures of unalterable law accept the ineluctable necessity of obedience, surrendering to the unopposable will.

The capitalist who 'knew' that the law of supply and demand was a universal law which must inevitably operate sooner or later and to which all social as well as all economic problems could be safely left, took refuge from an insoluble puzzle in a fatalistic reliance upon the will of fate. He was happy in the conviction that the capitalist system would overcome all its difficulties because the law of supply and demand was a universal law which nothing could successfully oppose. The prefascist revolutionaries, with a fatalism even more naïve, entrusted to the sacred laws of dialectical materialism the labors of a revolution they could not make themselves. And their successors, the fascists have carried the worship of fate to its last and most devout extreme. The fascists do not even trouble to translate their private destiny to terms of law. To them the sole duty of the individual is to surrender his will to the single will of his leader, who surrenders his will in turn to the mystical pulse of history. And the individual's sole destiny is to accept the inevitable future as the weeds accept the senseless and inevitable surging of a wave.

But it is not only in our political theories and our

historical theories and our economics that the men and
women of my generation are fatalists surrendering to
the will of fate. We have made the same confession
again and again in our literature. The books we have
written about ourselves and the world we live in are
books which will take their place in the great tradition
of such work. The best we have done is work well
done indeed; work which will be remembered. But
the picture of our world and of ourselves which these
books give is nevertheless a picture of a world compelled by forces beyond the control of men — a world
in which men at the worst are violated by these forces
and at the best are victims. The heroes of the books
we write about ourselves are neither heroes nor are
they masters of their fate: the very phrase for us has a
romantic, a pretentious, even a silly sound. The heroes
of the books we write about ourselves are defeated men
whom we pick out for notice because of the manner of
their defeat or because of their bravery in accepting it.
They are defeated men who have been defeated as the
martyrs were defeated, or defeated men who have accepted their defeat with the saving salve of irony, or
defeated men who have secretly escaped not only from
their defeat but from the world, or defeated men who
have revenged themselves on their defeat as a street boy
revenges himself upon the streets and buildings of his
city.

It is commonly said of the literature of my generation
that it is realistic, and for this it is much praised. It
deserves the praise, I think, but not the reason. Other
generations whose writers could claim an equal hon-

esty have presented a world which was at least as real
and altogether different. What is true of the characteristic novels of my generation is not that they are realistic
in any absolute or universal sense but that they are
realistic from a particular and special point of view —
which is the point of view of the defeated man, the
victim.

They are not so much realists' novels as they are victims' novels. The world they describe is the world as
the victim sees it. The truth they tell is the victim's
truth — the truth told behind the hand, the truth discreditable to the teller and the hearer — the low-down,
the confession, the exposure. The enemy of these
books also is the victim's enemy. The victim's enemy
is not the human enemy — another man or even many
other men. The victim is the figure crushed by forces
beyond his power to resist, unnameable forces often.
And so it is with the books we write about ourselves.
The enemy with us is something that rises out of the
total life of the time like the sour smoke that hangs over
a great city or something that rustles and gibbers and
mews in the contemporary psyche or something
sprawled along the whole of history, its tail and huge
hind quarters buried in the dark of long-past years.
The enemy is the System, or History itself or Life. The
truth of these books is the truth of the victims of this
enemy: the victims frustrated, thwarted, crippled and
destroyed.

It is a truth our generation has told as it has never
perhaps been told before — a truth our generation has
told in novels and plays and poems which surpass, as a

whole and as literature, the work of any other generation in this country. But the books in which this truth
is told are, nevertheless, books which mean, if they mean
anything, that our generation sees the world as the victim sees it, and accepts as unopposable and inescapable
the laws which take for us the place of fate.

It is for this reason, then, that the prophecies you
have heard are the prophecies of impotence and defeat.
They are the words of men who speak as prophets not
because they have greater knowledge of the future than
you but because they belong to a generation which believes that life is determined by a pre-existing pattern.
They are words of frustration and defeat because the
pattern of life in which their generation believes is a
fatalistic pattern: because their generation sees the
world as the victims of impersonal and mechanical
Laws, Necessities, and Systems see it.

It is for this reason also that you must be warned
against these speakers. Those who tell you that you
need not make decisions in this desperate time because
the laws of history will shape the future in any case,
those who tell you that you need not face the fact that
Naziism threatens everything you love because Naziism
is an agency of the historic process which will determine everything regardless of your acts — those who tell
you this are victims speaking consciously as victims in
a victim's words.

Those who tell you that the destroying guns, the
ruinous bombs, the fire, the misery, the indiscriminate
death of the fascist military action are a new, creative,
irresistible historic force which you cannot oppose but

only ride with as the rubbish rides the surf are victims
prophesying with the tongues of victims.

Those who tell you that you cannot defend democracy without losing it because the historic forces and
the economic laws will turn it into fascism the moment
you attempt to defend it; those who tell you that you
cannot win a war against fascism because the military
laws won't let you and that you will suffer humiliation
and disaster if you attempt to defend yourselves while
you still can, gaining honor and glory only if you sub-
mit — those who tell you this are victims shameless in
their cowardice as victims.

But it is not only because these speakers speak as
victims that you must be warned against them. You
must be warned against them because they are speakers
who are not disinterested speakers. Neither they nor
any others who accept the fatalism of historic necessity,
of universal law — neither they nor any others who
doubt the possibility of human action or the freedom
of the human will to act — are disinterested speakers.
Whether they so realize or not, they have taken sides
already in the basic conflict of our time. They are
men who would have been obliged to invent a fascist
revolution if they had not found one, and nothing they
may say in disapproval of the fascist method or the
fascist policy will change that fact. They have already
made and willingly made the one surrender which en-
genders all the rest. For the real issue is precisely the
issue between those, on the one side, who believe that
it is possible for men to imagine and by action to create
the kind of world they wish for — the kind of world in

which each man is truly free — and those, on the other side, who believe it is not possible for men to create for themselves the world they wish to live in but only possible to accept a world predestined, a world ordered and directed by those who know and will interpret the commands of fate. The real issue is the issue between those who believe in themselves and believe in their capacity to act and are willing to accept the responsibility for action, and those on the other who believe there is no room for men to act and no possibility that men will govern themselves and control their own lives and who therefore remit to the fates, to the universal laws, their responsibility for action.

Those who continue to believe, despite the failure of democracy to accomplish its ideal or even nearly to approach it in any country — those who continue to believe, despite the failures of democracy and the successes of the fascist armies, that man is what the Greeks believed him to be and what the founders of this republic believed him to be — will not accept the prophecies of defeated men. Neither will they accept the prophecies of those who offer to tell them how they can avoid the necessity of decision and of action. For they know, as they know nothing else on earth, that their first duty is to decide, and to decide with individual responsibility, and to decide with full and faithful knowledge of the facts. Only by such decision is government of the people by themselves conceivable.

Members of your generation, troubled by the prophecies, troubled also by the demands made upon your loyalties and your emotions from many sides, have ad-

dressed themselves in the last few months to men of my
generation demanding of us the answers to certain
questions of great difficulty and perplexity — demanding even that we supply you with certain convictions
which your education has not supplied: a central faith,
a central belief, which you now lack. It is understandable that you should ask but unlikely that your asking
will find answers. At least from us. The answers you
require are the answers which will enable you to believe
in your own lives and to respect your own hopes and to
accomplish your own purposes: the answers which will
enable you to take the great ambiguous words — democracy — liberty — humanity — freedom — and speak them
again as though you first had used them in the world;
the answers which will enable you to act and to believe.
Our generation has no such answers to supply. Ours
is a generation which never learned the answers you
have need of: a generation which inherited one set of
beliefs and threw them away because the world had
altered and took in their place the automatic laws, the
mechanical fatalities. It is not to us but to yourselves
that you must look for answers.

And it is in yourselves that you will find the answers.
You will remember, some of you, how Odysseus, seeking his way to his own life — his wife, his fruit trees, and
his island — beached his ship upon the foreshore of hell
to ask the prophet, Tiresias, for answers. You will remember also how he found among the dead there one
of his own men, Elpenor, a reckless and self-reliant man
who had gone on the roof of Circe's house to drink and
had fallen, breaking his neck bone.

You also, seeking your way to your own lives — you also will find upon this shadowy beach of time one of your own years who will answer you as Tiresias could never answer — one who will say as Elpenor would have said:

For myself — if you ask me —
There is no way back over sea-water

Nor by Earth's oaks or beyond them:
There is only the way on. . . .

You had best — trusting neither to
Charts nor to prophets but seamanship —

You had best — if you ask me —
Sail on by the sun to the seaward

Till you come to a clean place
With the smell of the pine in your faces and

Broom and a bitter turf
And the larks blown over the surf and the

Rocks red to the wave-height:
No sound but the wave's:

No call of a cock from the
Windward shore nor of oxen —

Gull's shadow for hawk's:
Gull's cry for the hawk's cry —

On by the open sea
To a land with a clean beach

An unplowed country
Pure under cleansing sun

With the dung burned dry on the gravel
And only the sand to have

And begin it again: start over....

You have only to cross this place
And launch ship and get way on her

Working her out with the oars to the
Full wind and go forward and

Bring yourselves to a home:
To a new land: to an ocean

Never sailed: not to Ithaca:
Not to your beds — but the withering

Seaweed under the thorn and the
Gulls and another morning.... [1]

[1] From *1933*, by Archibald MacLeish.

THE AMERICAN CAUSE

★

★

★

★

The American Cause

AN ADDRESS DELIVERED
AT FANEUIL HALL IN BOS-
TON, NOVEMBER 20, 1940

THE ISSUE before the American people is not a political issue nor an issue to be decided by a public act. It is an issue between the American people and themselves: an issue which involves the vitality and the resources of the American soul.

These, I am well aware, are large and ornate words. They are words which a man would have used at the risk of his reputation for sincerity a dozen months ago. But they are words which none of us can help but use today. History, not rhetoric, has put them in our mouths. History has shown us at late last that the issue

which divides our time is far more than an issue between armed forces. History has shown us that it is an
issue between worlds: an issue which depends more
surely on our souls than on our weapons: an issue
which no nation can avoid. Specifically and precisely,
history has made plain to us a fact we had refused before to see — the fact that the enemy which attacks us
attacks us not with planes alone or tanks alone or arms,
but with violence of belief. And the issue which the
people of this country face, the issue which lies between
this people and itself, is the issue whether or not those
who believe in democracy — those specifically who believe in democracy in the United States — can bring
against the violence and fanatical obsession of that in-
vading faith a stronger faith, a more resisting ardor of
their own.

Before the Battle of France — a battle which may
prove to have been more decisive in our own history
than in the history of Europe — fascism had seemed to
us a force of weapons driven onward by the fear of
force behind. But in the Battle of France we learned,
in the words of a manifesto issued by a group of the
most distinguished scholars in this country, that the
enemy 'were stronger in arms because they were
stronger in heart. It was their fanatical faith that gave
them wings and fire. It was the singleness of their purpose that quickened the spearhead of their march.' [1] In
France also we learned that the weakness of the democ-
racies — the weakness at least of the democracy which

---

[1] *The City of Man, a Declaration on World Democracy* (The Viking
Press, 1940).

there fell — was not, as we had wished to believe, a weakness only in arms, only in mechanical contrivances. We learned, in the words of the same manifesto, that the blindness of democratic diplomacy and the helplessness of democratic strategy 'were the external symptoms of a decay of the men. . . . This they called appeasement. It implied that no conviction is worth fighting for and that the boundaries between good and evil had fallen. Military defeat was the embodiment of moral abdication.'

It was the Battle of France which posed the issue we now face. Before that battle we had thought ourselves spectators of a war in Europe. After it, we knew the war was not in Europe but nearer — in the darker and more vulnerable countries of men's hearts. And after it we were not certain it was we who were spectators.

But the Battle of France did more than pose this issue. It weighted it — and weighted it against us. Before the Battle of France we had not understood — as a nation we had not understood — that the vitality of our democratic faith was put in issue. After the Battle of France we feared the issue was already lost. We saw then that the war was not, as we had wished to believe, a war between European powers which wanted conflicting things but a war between human beings who believed conflicting things. We saw that the differences of belief were differences as to the kind of society in which men should live. We saw that those who believed in the kind of society in which we also believe had been opposed not only by weapons, not only by machines, but by other men who believed, and believed

fanatically, in the total destruction of that society. We
saw that in the fighting which followed it had been those
who believed fanatically in destruction who had been
stronger and those who believed in the society in which
we believe who had been less strong — less strong not
only in their weapons but in their devotion to their
cause. And we had wondered. We wondered whether
the sickness of democracy in France would prove to be
the sickness of democracy in every country. We wondered whether democracy, which had been unable to
match conviction with conviction and certainty with
certainty in France, would be able to match conviction
with conviction elsewhere. We still are wondering. We
are wondering whether democracy in the United States
has other spiritual weapons than the doubts and mis-
givings which ten years of depression and twenty years
of skepticism provided for the men of France to fight
with.

It is of this fear I wish to speak. And to speak as
candidly and earnestly as I am capable of speaking. It
is a fear which exists — and which exists in the minds
not of foolish or of frightened people, but of responsible
men who love this country as well as any of its people
love it. It is also an understandable fear, for events
which all of us have witnessed make it understandable.
It is not a fear therefore which scornful men can put
aside, or which demagogues can shout down, or which
the patriotic societies can suppress with resolutions. It
is a fear of which we must take account. But it is nevertheless — or so at least it seems to me — a fear both
needless and mistaken. For it rests upon a total mis-

conception of the democratic cause. It rests, to be precise, upon the misconception of democracy which those who most despise democracy have done their best to propagate and broadcast through the world. It is the fear of those who, being democrats themselves, accept the definition of democracy their enemies have written.

The enemies of liberty are not saboteurs in material things alone. They are saboteurs also in the things of the mind. And it is in the things of the mind that their sabotage is most dangerous. To destroy a machine or a manufacturing plant is one thing. The loss is great but the plant or the machine is replaceable. To destroy the integrity of words and to destroy the credibility of the users of words is another; neither can be replaced. The enemies of liberty, here as in other countries, practice the destruction of the integrity of words and the destruction of the credibility of the users of words. Indeed, it is this practice which principally characterizes the enemies of freedom in our time. They are the first men — the first men in the five hundred years since Johannes Gutenberg zum Jungen, Knight of Mainz, invented the art of printing — the first man to use the printing press, deliberately and systematically, as an instrument of confusion and deceit. They are the first men in the five centuries of printing to turn the printing presses, like machine guns, on the people.

And nowhere have they used these *Kulturwaffen* to destroy a word more skillfully than with the word 'democracy'— the word essential to our cause — the word which *is* our cause — the word we must defend whatever else we lose, or fail to fight for, or do not defend.

What the enemies of liberty would have us take the word 'democracy' to mean is not what Adams thought it meant, or Jefferson, or those who took it westward through the Shenandoah, or those who came to find it here by shipload after shipload through a hundred years. What the enemies of liberty would have us take the word to mean is something men and money and machines created in the nineteenth century and *called* democracy — a way of owning property, a scheme of doing business, an opportunity for comfort or for power or for certain forms of gain or entertainment.

It is this the enemies of liberty would have us take the word to mean. And it is with this meaning in our minds that they would have us make the choice before us — a choice, they say, between the new oncoming order of their fascist world and an old corrupted system full of fat and death — a choice between the new and iron cause for which a people can forget itself and sacrifice itself and go without and suffer and if need be die, and, on the other side, a world of goods and things and comforts and amusements with nothing to believe in but more goods, more things.

This was the choice which their confusions and their defamations and deceits presented to the citizens of France — and which the citizens of France, duped by confusions and deceits, accepted. It is the choice which many in this country, duped or themselves the dupers, would accept as well. The diplomat who tells us that democracy is dead in England, meaning by democracy a way of trading stocks, a chance to make ten millions in the market, accepts the choice the citizens of France accepted. The famous woman who assures us in a beautiful and cadenced prose that democracy is old in every country, and that the future like a wave will drown it down, accepts the same alternatives of terror and despair.

But the fears and desperations and defeats which these and others like them breed and scatter are unreal fears. The democracy of which this writer and this statesman speak is not democracy but a distorted lie which both, but for their different reasons, take for true. Democracy itself has never been and is not now and never can become a way of trade, a world of goods, a heap of products, whether those products are of gold or steel or corn or silk or what-not: whether the trade is large or small or free or planned or neither. And only a very foolish man — only a man who had no understanding of the word 'democracy,' or what it had been once, or what it can be — would take the issue in these terms and let his enemies compel him to defend, not the dream of freedom in the mind, not the way of freedom toward the future, but things already made, systems established, ways of trading, heaps of goods piled up.

If democracy is what the fascists say it is — if democracy is nothing but the world of innumerable automobiles and the best telephone system on earth and a new gadget just around the corner and the radios driveling on in the hotel lobbies eighteen hours out of twenty-four and the simpering legs in the magazine advertisements and the simpering voices on the movie screen and the hundreds of thousands of miles of roadside

billboards with the billboard faces and the ten millions
of unemployed waiting for the next boom — if democracy is only this, then democracy cannot survive attack,
for democracy is not a cause that men will fight for.

But the true issue is not this issue; democracy is not
the world that men and money and machines built in
the nineteenth century and called democracy. The
real issue is an issue to be fought in the hard and stony
passes of the human spirit — the strict Thermopylaes
of time where even if a man is killed he cannot die.
And democracy itself is neither things nor goods nor
fatness and indifference and an empty heart, but winter
on the Massachusetts Bay and cold at Trenton and the
gunfire in Kentucky and the hungry ground. The real
issue is an issue between the frenzy on the one side of
a herded, whipped-up, crowd-begotten 'cause,' and on
the other side the single man's belief in liberty of mind
and spirit; his willingness to sacrifice his goods and
comforts and his earnings for its sake.

The democratic faith which swept the world — the
democratic faith which men believed in and men fought
for, the faith which men believe in and will fight for
still, is not a faith in things or goods or fortunes. John
Milton knew the democratic faith that men will fight
for. He spoke of it not once but often:

'And as for you, citizens, it is of no small concern,
what manner of men ye are, whether to acquire, or to
keep possession of your liberty. Unless your liberty be
of that kind which can neither be gotten nor taken
away by arms (and that alone is such which springing
from piety, justice, temperance, in fine from real virtue,

shall take deep and intimate root in your minds) you
may be assured that there will not be wanting one, who,
even without arms, will speedily deprive you of what
it is your boast to have gained by force of arms. . . .
For know (that you may not feel resentment, or be
able to blame anybody but yourselves), that as to be
free is precisely the same thing as to be pious, wise, just
and temperate, careful of one's own, abstinent from
what is another's, and thence in fine, magnanimous and
brave — so to be the opposite of these, is the same thing
as to be a slave; and by the wonted judgment and as it
were by the just retribution of God, it comes to pass,
that the nation, which has been incapable of governing
and ordering itself, and has delivered itself up to the
slavery of its own lusts, is itself delivered over against
its will to other masters — and whether it will or no is
compelled to serve.'

John Milton's democracy was a democracy in which
men believed. It was a democracy for which a band of
sober and unmilitary men fought as armies had not
fought before them. It was a faith more powerful than
any faith or cause which could be brought against it. It
has been a faith more powerful than any other for three
centuries of time and on two continents. It is still a
faith more powerful than any other. All our history
has made this plain. Whenever in the history of this
nation we have given ourselves to the labor of creating
upon this continent a life in which every man might
have the freedom of his mind, we have been confident
and certain of our future and assured and asked no
questions either of ourselves or anyone. Whenever we

have given ourselves to other labors, we have lost the
meaning of our lives and lost our certainty and questioned everyone and most of all ourselves.

Three generations back in the thirties and the forties
of the last century when the four-hundred-foot side-
wheelers with the crystal chandeliers and the mahogany
bars and eight-course dinners and the filigree funnels
with their sparks like crazy stars went hooting and slap-
ping up the Ohio and the Hudson and the Mississippi,
the American had no questions about democracy. They
had a job to do. They had the toughest job a people
ever undertook — the job of clearing and settling and
tying together with ships and roads and rails and words
and names the largest area lived on as a single social
unit by any nation, at any time. They had the job of
creating on an undiscovered continent a country where
a hundred million men could live in freedom from the
rest and from each other. They had the actual and
present job of clearing on this continent the quarter
sections where a man could build his freedom out of
logs and nails.

And while they had that job to do they asked no
questions. They knew what democracy was. They
knew what they were too. They were the smartest,
toughest, luckiest, leanest, all-around knowingest nation
on God's green earth. Their way of living was the
handsomest way of living human being had ever hit on.
Their institutions were the institutions history had
been waiting for. If you had told them anyone else
had a harder hold on the earth than they had, or anyone else believed in himself more than they believed in

themselves, they would have laughed in your face. And gone on with their working.

Who they were, what they were, never bothered the Americans. Virginia gentlemen and Boston philosophers and Long Island poets and visiting British lecturers might write and talk and wonder about American manners and American origins and American politics and the American soul. Americans didn't wonder. They knew all about them. They knew about origins. They had all the origins of Europe in their veins before the century was over — all the races a man ever heard of and a lot more beside. Races didn't bother the Americans. They were something a lot better than any race. They were a People. They were the first self-constituted, self-declared, self-created People in the history of the world. And their manners were their own business. And so were their politics. And so, but ten times so, were their souls.

Who an American was and what democracy was, was nothing to talk about. You could see for yourself. An American was a man who had the luck to be born on this continent where the heat was hotter and the cold was colder and the sun was brighter and the nights were blacker and the distances were farther and the faces were nearer and the rain was more like rain and the mornings were more like mornings than anywhere else on earth — sooner and sweeter and lovelier over unused hills.

An American was a man who knew which way to take to reach tomorrow. An American was a man who could let himself in and let himself out and nobody asking him 'please,' not even the President. An American was a man who never asked anyone anything — who he was or where he came from or what he did — because it was answer enough to be a man. At least in America.

That was the way it used to be in this country. That was the way it was while the people of this country were clearing the quarter sections for a free man's field. That is the way it has been whenever we have remembered clearly and understood with reality what democracy is.

For democracy is never a thing done. Democracy is always something that a nation must be doing. The quarter sections which were freedom a hundred years ago are now not freedom. Freedom will be somewhere else. But the labor of creating freedom is the same. And the consequence.

What is necessary now is one thing and one thing only — that the issue of democracy be made precise and clear — that democracy become again democracy in action, not democracy accomplished and piled up in goods and gold.

Democracy in action is a cause for which the stones themselves will fight.

DIVIDED WE FALL

★
★
★
★

Divided We Fall

ADDRESS DELIVERED AT THE IN-
AUGURAL DINNER OF FREEDOM
HOUSE, MARCH 19, 1942

IF AMERICAN OPINION is determined that this war shall be won, it will be won. No Pacific or North African or European defeat can be final. No reverse anywhere in the world can be more than a temporary setback. American man-power, American skill, American production, backed by a fixed and unalterable American resolution, will survive all such misfortunes and inevitably win. For a determined and unrelenting and powerful America will rally not only itself but all who fight beside it, holding together in one convinced and unconquerable force the freedom-loving peoples of the world.

But if American opinion is not determined, if the American people are not committed entirely and irrevocably to a complete and final victory, this war can be lost. Any defeat, anywhere in the world, however far away, can be a major disaster. American man-power, American skill, American production, backed by an irresolute and divided American purpose, will never be brought to bear upon the enemy; will be half-used or unused; will rally no one — not even the Americans themselves.

Our enemies know this. Our enemies have known it for a long time. From the beginning of the war in Europe, even long before the beginning of the war in Europe, the Nazis sought to prepare the terrain of this American battlefield for their own maneuver. They attempted by their own propaganda, and by the assistance of their friends and their dupes within the United States, to ditch and divide and tunnel and undermine the field of common American opinion. They sought to fence and hedge it off with doubts — doubts as to the strength of our democratic institutions — doubts as to the efficiency of representative government — doubts as to the validity of equal rights before the law — doubts as to the possibility and wisdom of religious and racial tolerance in the contemporary world.

They played upon the natural political differences which, in the American past, have been elements of American strength. They played upon them until they had turned political differences into personal passions — until campaigns of normal political opposition had become in certain quarters and in certain mouths cam-

paigns of private slander and insidious abuse aimed at
the destruction of confidence in the elected officers of
the people — and thus at the destruction of confidence
in elected government itself.

Above all they attempted to divide the ground of
American opinion along social and religious lines, as
they had already divided the ground of European
opinion in preparation for European conquest. They
sought to persuade the well-meaning people of this
country, as they had already persuaded the well-meaning people of Europe, that the war the Nazis were themselves fomenting was actually a vast and inevitable civil
war which no country could avoid — a civil war dividing every man in every country from his neighbor —
dividing the rich man from the poor man, the liberal
from the conservative, the Protestant from the Catholic,
the white man from the black, the Jew from the Gen-
tile — and dividing them, not by mere differences of
opinion, such differences as Americans have known
and tolerated and resolved for generations, but dividing
them by some fierce and unavoidable and inexplicable
distinction which only blood and civil murder and civil
persecution could resolve. Picking up where the American Communists with their solemn and ineffectual
antics, their stilted jargon and their schoolboy plots, had
failed, the Nazis and the Fascists of 1938 and 1939 and
1940 attempted to build their barricades across the
American mind, dig their tunnels of slander and suspicion and mistrust beneath the levels of American tolerance and good sense.

Their strategy, now that the war is made, follows the

tactics of the preparation. The military operation has a propaganda purpose. Believing, as they do, that the divisions they have done their best to create in American opinion are divisions so profound, so irremediable, that the common American purpose cannot survive external pressure of any kind — the pressure of remote defeats, the pressure of inevitable withdrawals — believing this, the Axis strategists have mapped their course accordingly. The pincers of Axis attack in the Pacific and Atlantic are pointed not at our coasts so much as at our courage. Axis strategy has for its objectives in these next few critical months not only the world's supplies of oil, not only the world's strategic fortresses, but the minds and hearts of the people of this country. Axis strategy, that is to say, is based in large part upon the contemptuous belief that such a people as we are, of many origins, of many faiths, brought up for generations in the love of tolerance and the respect for other men's opinions, can never maintain a common fighting purpose under the pressure of the war they mean to make.

It is for this reason that the struggle to fix and to maintain American determination is the crucial struggle of this year. If we Americans can win that battle, no other loss will matter. If we lose it, no victories, now or in the months to come, will right the balance. But it is a victory we, the American people, must win for ourselves and a victory we can only win by fighting for it. Little the government can say or do *as government* can effect the outcome. Earnest and deeply troubled people who see this battlefield for what it is and understand the danger, have called upon the officers of government in Washington for action. Columnists and professional advisers of the public mind have urged officers of government in Washington to do this or to do that — to provide more news or different news, better news or worse news — to speak more often or less often — with more authority or less authority — or merely in some other style. Some of these suggestions have been intelligent; some have not. Some should be acted on; some should never have been heard. But none of them, not the best or wisest, touches the question at its heart.

In the battle for American opinion it is the American people, and not their government, who alone can make the fight. The government of a dictatorship will tell its people what to think and will employ every means at its disposal to prevent their thinking thoughts it does not like. But it is principally for that reason that free men hate dictatorship. The government of a democracy, by virtue of its existence as a democratic government, has a very different function in relation to the making of opinion. Its function is to see to it that the people have the facts before them — the facts on which opinions can be formed.

In time of war it is a difficult function to perform. Certain of the facts — certain of the most important facts — have military significance and can be published to the people of the country only in such forms or with such delays as will not provide the enemy with information. But the duty of government nevertheless remains: to see to it that the people have the necessary facts before them — the facts about the war itself, about the enemy, his purposes, the consequences of defeat; the facts about the enemy's methods and particularly the enemy's disguises — his hidden methods in propaganda and in espionage; the facts about the plans and purposes of the people's government in its prosecution of the war, particularly the government's plans which call upon the people for participation or for self-denial.

But beyond that, the formation of opinion in a democracy in wartime, as in time of peace, is a labor for the people — a labor no one but the people can perform. It is for the men and women of this country, who understand the meaning of the facts before them, to fight for the common purpose in which they all believe — to fight against the divisive opinion, the destructive opinion, which would defeat that purpose. It is for the men and women who understand the true nature of Naziism and Fascism — who know what it would really mean to lose this war — to struggle individually, or in their organizations, *for* the forging of a common national determination, *against* the enemies who would defeat the common will.

It is not an easy struggle, but it is a struggle which can certainly be won. The first necessity here, as in any war, is to identify the enemy. But here the identification of the enemy is not difficult. The enemy in this struggle for the American mind is any man or any woman who attempts by any means to break or to defeat or frustrate the determination of this people to fight this war through to an absolute and final victory.

The enemy, therefore, is not only the Axis propagandist — the Iowa Lord Haw-Haw hamming on the

short-wave radio or the sniveling Japanese professor
with the Berkeley accent — but the whole unsavory crew
of Nazi and Fascist Japanese panders and deceivers
and distorters of the truth.

The enemy is also the American defeatist who would
rather lose the war, and with it everything America has
been or can become, than make the terrible effort victory demands — the idle women whose dinner hours
have been altered and who call their country's struggle
for its life 'this wretched war'; the sluggish men on the
commuters' trains who have never fought for anything
but golf-balls in their lives and who do not propose to
begin at this late hour; the slippery whisperers in the
press and in the hotel lobbies who know the meaning
of American defeat — and want it — and who know well
why they want it.

The enemy is the American divisionist: the American
who fears or hates our allies in this war more than he
trusts and loves his fellow citizens — the American bigot
who fears the beliefs of the Russian people more than
he trusts the beliefs of the people of America, and who
would willingly see the United States destroyed if
Russia could be destroyed in the same disaster — the
American patriot whose patriotism is directed not to
the United States but to the country of his European
origin — the American with the ineradicable immigrant
mentality who would rather see this country over-
whelmed than see it aided by a nation his father or his
grandfather once hated in another country and another
time.

The enemy is the American partisan who would win

his partisan victories at any cost of suffering or defeat to
his own country: the newspaper publisher to whom
treason itself is not detestable if by treason he can injure those he hates — the vindictive politician who
would pay his scores off in his country's blood — the
reckless and revengeful few who would not hesitate to
strike the object of their passion across their children's
bodies and their nation's shame.

It is a malodorous and contemptible company of enemies — a company bound together not by love of anything but by hatred of many things — a company having
only this in common: that it loves this country and this
country's peoples less than it loves its private hatreds
and its private spleen.

These and such as these are the enemies in this battle.
But they are the enemies not of the government of the
United States, not of the present administration, not of
any officer of the administration, but of the people
themselves.

The man who attempts, through his ownership of a
powerful newspaper, to dictate the opinions of millions
of Americans — the man who employs all the tricks and
dodges of a paid propaganda to undermine the people's
confidence in their leaders in a war, to infect their
minds with suspicion of their desperately needed allies,
to break their will to fight, is the enemy, not of the
government of this country, but of its people — and,
most of all, the people he deceives the most, his readers.
The politician who serves for years as the principal
propagandist of the notion that this country is secure
from all attack, and who later, when attack occurs, gloats

at his country's losses saying, 'I told you so,' 'I told you
so,' is the enemy, not of the administration or its officers,
but of the people he has misled once and would again.

Nothing would please these enemies more than to
pass as enemies of the government only, or of some
officer of government. Nothing would please them
more than to persuade the country that they were
merely political opponents of a man or a few men in
public life. For then any remonstrance, any reply, any
resistance to their operations, could be written off as
political partisanship. The free election of a free people
could be used by enemies of the people's freedom to
camouflage their actual purpose — to provide their propaganda with a limitless immunity, a perfect and impenetrable disguise.

It would not be the first time that democratic institutions had been used for such an end.

I do not think the trick will be successful in America.
I do not think the people of America will be deceived.
I think the people of this country recognize their ene-
mies and will confront them. I think the will of the
Americans will hold in spite of lies, in spite of hate, in
spite of treason.

I think the just indignation of a great people, aroused
by unbearable outrage to a terrible anger, will fight this
war through to the final end.

I think that end will be our victory: absolute and
conclusive and our own.

WASHINGTON IS AMERICA

★

★

★

★

Washington Is America

ADDRESS DELIVERED BEFORE THE
NATIONAL RETAIL DRY GOODS
ASSOCIATION, JUNE 17, 1942

FROM THE BEGINNING of the republic one of the inalienable American rights has been the right to cuss the government. Life, liberty, and the pursuit of Congressmen, they used to say in the old-time country newspapers. Maybe they still do. But whether they do or not the principle still stands. It's a man's right, if he governs himself, to say what he thinks of his handiwork. It's a free man's right, an American's right, to climb up on the next stump and tell the world how the government looks from there. Some would say it's the dearest right a free man has. Certainly it's the last right most of us would willingly surrender. It's a right we're jealous of in these United States.

We're jealous of it because it is not only a free man's right; it is *the* free man's right — the right which, more than any other, distinguishes the man who has freedom from the man who hasn't. And for two reasons. First, because the free man is the only man who *can* enjoy the privilege. And, second, because the free man is the only man who knows *how* to enjoy it — because its exercise is, in a sense, the mark of the free man. Of the two, the second is more important than the first. As certain events of the last few months have made painfully clear. When you hear those who aren't free, or those who hate freedom, or those who aim to destroy freedom, trying to imitate the free man's lambasting of his government you get a rough but sufficient idea of the importance of knowing how to do it. You get an idea which may stay with you for a long time.

When a free man sails into his government he sails into it partly because he doesn't like it but mostly because it's his. He cusses it the way you cuss a mean relation. But when a man who doesn't know the way of freedom, who hasn't learned the feel and sense of freedom, sails into a free man's government he doesn't talk about it as though it were his. He doesn't cuss it from inside the family or from next door. He cusses it from the outside and with an outside feeling — with an outside animosity. What he says is as awkward and wrong and in some ways as comical as Brooklyn talk in the Wyoming cow country. But it's not comical altogether or awkward only. It can be dangerous too.

It can be dangerous primarily for this reason: that its effect, if you get enough of it, can be to infect others — even others who have the real sense and feel of freedom — with the notion that their government, their free men's government, isn't actually theirs but is something outside them, something, even, *against* them. Its effect, if you get enough of it, can be to break down and injure and perhaps eventually destroy the most precious thing free men have — the thing which is, in the last analysis, the touchstone of their freedom — that sense of identity with their government — their sense that their government is theirs — is *them*. Destroy that sense and you destroy the reality of self-government leaving the form only. Destroy self-government and there is very little freedom left.

A free man's right to cuss his government, in other words, is a right which must be guarded as closely in the practice as in the possession. And it is for that reason that men who value freedom are so jealous of it. It is for that reason that men who value freedom resent its abuse more bitterly than most abuses of their rights. They realize that the abuse of the right can not only corrupt the right but injure the structure itself on which their freedom rests. They realize that a Bertie McCormick or a whole family of Bertie McCormicks who abuse the free man's right by pumping out a vast and costly propaganda aimed to persuade the people to hate and fear their government and their President are violating the basic decencies of a free man's world. And they are not impressed when they are told that the McCormick family is doing nothing more than to exercise

the sacred right of 'criticism.'   The people of this country know all about criticism.   They know about Bertie
McCormick too.   And they know where the one ends
and the other begins.

Criticism in a free man's country is made on certain
assumptions, one of which is the assumption that the
government belongs to the people and is at all times
subject to the people's correction and criticism — correction and criticism such as a man gives, and should give,
those who represent him and undertake to act on his
behalf.   Criticism of the government made upon that
basis is proper criticism, no matter how abusive.   But
abuse of a representative government made not upon
that assumption but upon the assumption that the government is one thing and the people another — that the
President is one thing and the people who elected the
President another — that the Congress is one thing and
the people who elected the Congress another — that the
executive departments are one thing and the people
whom the departments serve another — abuse of a representative government made with the implication that
the government is something outside the people, or
opposed to the people, something the people should
fear and hate — abuse of that kind is not 'criticism'
and no amount of editorial self-justification can make
it sound as though it were.   It is a harmful propaganda.   And a propaganda which is no less harmful because it is untrue.

For it is untrue.   The picture of Washington — and
it is a picture found not only in the propaganda press
but in the newspapers devoted to news as well — the

picture of Washington as another nation, almost a
foreign power, fixed upon our shores to wage a kind of
bureaucratic war upon our people, is a picture which
would be fantastic if it were not so frequently presented. Who are these Congressmen and Senators who
are now set off in apparent distinction from the American people? They *are* the American people. They are
the people's representatives in Congress elected by the
people and acting in the people's behalf. Like the
people whom they represent they are men of varying
degrees of ability, varying and various opinions. Some
of them are men of great distinction. Some are not.
Some are men of an intelligence as fine and as responsive as any to be found in America. Some are men of
less intelligence. Some are men remarkable for courage
and character. Some are not remarkable for any reason.
But one thing is true of them all as they constitute the
Congress of the United States: they are the true representatives of the people whom they represent and much
more like the people, far closer to the people, much
more truly entitled to speak for the people, than those
who undertake to attack them on the people's behalf.
It would not be possible to assemble anywhere in the
United States five hundred and thirty-one men and
women who could more justly and more humanly speak
for the people of this republic than the five hundred
and thirty-one men and women whom the people have
elected to Congress precisely for that purpose.

And what is true of the Congress is true also of the
alleged bureaucracy — a new word incidentally in
American usage — new since the last war and generally

used only in the past few years. Members of this Association, like members of similar associations throughout the country, have reason to know the truth about
the bureaucrats who figure as a hostile army in the
propaganda prints and in the reckless statements of
those who take the propaganda prints for truth. Who
are these wartime bureaucrats who are said to stand on
one side while the American people (or the American
laborer or the American retailer) stand on the other?
Who are these wartime bureaucrats who make up a
wartime government different and distinct from the
American people? Who are they indeed but your own
colleagues, your own associates, people like yourselves
who have given up their jobs, given up their homes and
businesses, separated themselves from their families and
their friends — and for what reason? For one reason
only — to do their duty as citizens: to get the job done:
to win this war.

Who are these bureaucrats? Don Nelson? Bill Batt?
Is Bob Patterson a bureaucrat, who gave up a place on
the Federal Bench to work sixteen and eighteen hours
a day at less pay and with the dead certainty that he
would be crucified in the end if anything went wrong?
Is Milo Perkins a bureaucrat, who left a profitable
business in Texas because he thought there was a job
in Washington which had to be done — and who almost
killed himself in the doing of it? Is Jerry Land a
bureaucrat, who could have retired at the conclusion of
a distinguished Navy career, but who has kept on to
build the ships we need to win the war — and more
ships — and yet more ships until there is no time to

sleep or eat? Is Leon Henderson a bureaucrat, who has taken on the toughest and most unpopular job in America — the job of fixing prices and rationing essential goods to peg down the big top when the inflationary gale begins to blow: is a man a bureaucrat who starts his conferences at half-past six in the morning and ends them well after midnight at a salary an assistant treasurer would sniff at and with nothing ahead but more of the same for a long time coming? Are Jack McCloy and Bob Lovett bureaucrats, who left a law practice and a big bank in New York to take on two of the most thankless assignments in Washington at an assistant secretary's pay with the knowledge that the world would only hear of either of them if the job went wrong — Jack McCloy and Bob Lovett, who have turned in two of the great performances of this war. Is Elmer Davis a bureaucrat — Elmer Davis, who has given up one of the sweetest and surest and most peaceful jobs in journalism to take on a government chore in which — and I speak of something of which I have a certain knowledge — in which the only sure reward is public vilification and private hurt? Is Henry Stimson a bureaucrat — Henry Stimson, who had won all the honors his country had to give him? Is Frank Knox? Henry Morgenthau? Cordell Hull?

And if not these, then who? The tens and scores and hundreds of American business men and American lawyers and American scientists and American engineers who are working in Washington at sixty-five hundred or fifty-six hundred or thirty-eight hundred a year, living in hot rooms in back hotels and maybe a sight of their wives every seven weeks with their kids forgetting their faces? And for what? For cash? For fame? Or to get the job done.

You will forgive me if I say that the whole picture of Washington as a bureaucracy distinct from the American people strikes me as pretty cheap — contemptible and cheap. I hold no brief for the city. There are other places I would rather live and would live if I could. I hold no brief for the people in it either. There are quite a lot I'd send back to the towns they came from if I had the sending. But this much I do know — that the newspaper picture, the magazine picture, of a foreign, bureaucratic Washington, hostile to the people of this country, putting its own interests before their interests — a bureaucratic Washington distinct from the people, separate from the people — is a pure and unadulterated invention.

There *is* no such Washington. What there actually is, is a city filled with American citizens — American citizens from all over, from every state — American citizens like other American citizens — American citizens who have closed their offices, turned their businesses over, locked up their laboratories and their shops, said good-bye to their wives and gone to work in the most uncomfortable, overcrowded city in the United States at half or a fifth or a hundredth of their civilian incomes — gone to work at low pay in the worst climate on the continent with no more hope or expectation of recognition or reward than a stevedore has on the night shift.

That's your bureaucracy. It stares at you every night from the lighted windows still lit at ten and eleven and twelve in Lend-Lease, in the War Department, the Treasury, OPA, WPB, the House Office Building, the Senate Office Building, even — forgive me — the Library. It stares at you every morning in the long lines of cars on Memorial Bridge at eight and at seven-thirty and seven and on back. That's your bureaucratic Washington. And the marvel is that the Washington correspondents, the ablest correspondents of the ablest press on earth, have never written the story. It's under their noses. They see it every day. It's a better story than the gossip and the guesses. And yet they've never written it. And since they've never written it the editors and the columnists and the magazine publishers back home go on from week to week with the talk about bureaucrats, the talk about bureaucratic confusion, the talk about talk. You can still find a cool apartment up in New York to write the wise-cracks in. You can still drop down to the office at ten and stay until five and think up a couple of cracks about bureaucrats. And all the confusion in Washington. And the way the people in Washington get excited about the war. You can still find a seat in a bar in New York about six o'clock for a long drink and a laugh at the fools down in Washington.

Why the true story hasn't been told I don't know. I suppose there are fashions in news like fashions in other things. But this much I do know — that if the true story of Washington were told it would bury forever the propaganda which tries to set the American Gov-

ernment over against the American people. Washington these days is more like America than America itself.
It is filled with America — filled and overfilled to over-
flowing with America. There are more Americans —
more kinds of Americans — more samples of Americans
in Washington than there are anywhere else on earth.
There are Americans from all towns, Americans from
all the trades. And the towns and the trades know it
if the newspapers don't. You know it — people in your
trades. Members of your association, representatives of
your businesses spend night after night, day after day in
Washington, one week after the other. You know precisely how grotesque it is to picture Washington as a
bureaucracy separate and distinct from the life of the
rest of the country. You know — your representatives
know — how frequently they were called down for
council — how long the hours were they kept. You
know, too, how often the people in Washington with
whom you had to do were your own former colleagues,
men from your own profession, your own trades.

The truth of the matter is — and it is, to me at least,
a very moving truth — that the organization of the
American people to fight this war is an organization
chiefly remarkable for the fact that there *is* no bureaucracy in the European sense — that there *is* no such distinction between the people and their government as
the propaganda pretends. If there ever was a wartime
government truly responsive to a self-governing people,
it is this government. If there ever was a government
which represented the people because it *was* the people,
it is the government in Washington. And this is due,

not only to the insistence of a great and greatly democratic President, but equally to the insistence of the
people themselves. It is due, to be specific, to the devotion and responsibility of just such organizations as
this — organizations of citizens who put their duties as
citizens before their interests as men of business.

THE POWER OF THE BOOK

★
★
★
★

The Power of the Book

ADDRESS DELIVERED BEFORE THE
AMERICAN BOOKSELLERS ASSOCI-
ATION, MAY 6, 1942

THIS MEETING is almost an anniversary. It lacks four days of being the ninth anniversary of the Nazi bonfire of May 10, 1933, in which twenty-five thousand books were burned.

I mention that fact not because historical coincidence is particularly important — not because the day of the bonfire of books in Berlin was the tenth of May and the day of this booklovers' dinner in New York is the sixth — but because both occasions were remarkable for the same reason: both were tributes to the power of the book.

More particularly I mention them together because, in a certain and very compelling sense, the bonfire of Berlin was the greater — if unintended — tribute. And because certain consequences follow from that fact.

The Nazis — the misled and ignorant boys, the frustrated generation which made up the Nazi rabble, which became the Nazi gang, which produced the Nazi 'Order'— these Nazis perpetrated their obscene and spiteful act because they knew, ignorant and disappointed and defeated as they were, that books are weapons and that a free man's books — such books as free men with a free man's pride can write — are weapons of such edge and weight and power that those who would destroy the world of freedom must first destroy the books that freedom fights with.

The question I should like to pose to you tonight — the question all of us who live with books, writers as well as booksellers, publishers as well as librarians, professors as well as public servants, must pose to ourselves — is this: Do we, for all our protestations — do we, for all our talk of books and all our labor with books and all our knowledge of books — do we recognize the power of books as truly as the Nazi mob which dumped them on a fire — do we truly and actually, in our lives as well as in our words, ascribe as great an influence to the books we write and publish and sell and catalogue and teach, as those who fear the free men's books enough to burn them?

I am not indulging in rhetoric. I am asking a question. And I am asking it with the greatest seriousness of which I am capable. I think I know the answer. I

think you know it too. But you will agree with me
that a Devil's advocate could give us, if he wished, an
uncomfortable half-hour.

A competent Devil's advocate could ask us to forget
the brutality and ignorance of the Nazis for a moment
and think back over our own behavior in the last decades
to say whether, in our honest judgment, we who dealt
with books during this period had acted as though we
thought of books as powerful influences — as instruments by which the lives of men and nations can be
shaped — or whether, on the contrary, we thought of
books as merchandise — as packages to be sold alongside
of rubber toothbrushes and bottles of hair tonic and
packages of proprietary pills. It would not be an easy
question to answer. We could reply in all honesty that
the methods of merchandizing developed in the twenties and practiced in the thirties sold quantities of books
such as had never before been sold and carried best-
seller after best-seller over previous best-seller records
until there seemed to be no limit to possible best-seller
sales. But our Devil's advocate, when we told him we
had sold such quantities of books, could ask, 'What
books?' 'And selected for sale by what standards?' 'And
to what effect?'

'Certainly,' he could say to us, 'all questions of literary merit aside' — and I assume we should be only too
happy to leave them aside — 'all questions of literary
merit aside, there was as little in these books themselves
as in your handling of these books to indicate that you
thought of books as powerful influences on the nation's
life or on the nation's future. If ever the people of a

great nation were ignorant of the secret changes of the
world in which they lived — if ever the people of a
great nation were unprepared to face the gathering and
unfamiliar dangers of a changing time — the people of
this country were ignorant and unprepared when first
the Nazis struck for power. A few books on the best-
seller lists — books like Hemingway's *For Whom the
Bell Tolls* — books like Ed Taylor's *Strategy of Terror*
— books like Bill Shirer's *Diary* — were books about the
actual world — books which, if believed, would have
given the people of the country some understanding of
the dangers they faced before those dangers materialized
in bombers over Honolulu and dead men off the Atlantic Coast. But the great bulk of the book sales were
sales of books which gave no indication whatever of the
actualities of our time — no indication that the history
of the last ten years has been a history which could only
end in mortal danger to ourselves — no indication that
the fascist revolution in Spain was the beginning of a
fascist war which put our lives also, our freedoms also,
in mortal peril, or that the Nazi conquest of Czecho-
slovakia was a conquest aimed, not at the Bohemian
mountains only, but at other and more distant countries and eventually our own.'

There is no reason to push the imaginary colloquy
further or to make the obvious debaters' points on the
other side: the point that American writers as a group
were the earliest and the most courageous fighters
against fascism in this country, exposing the Franco
revolution in Spain for what it was when few besides
the writers were willing to do so; the point that many

American publishers devoted more time and money than they had to spare to the publication of anti-fascist books; the point that there were booksellers who undertook as a patriotic duty the forewarning of the people. All of these points can be made and others besides. But the fact nevertheless remains that the record as a whole is not a record of effective use of books for a purpose for which books could have been, and should have been, effective.

All of us, I think, will now agree that the American record over the last two decades is not a satisfying record. All of us will agree that the chain of folly linked to folly leads back from the tragic day when Bataan surrendered — the tragic day of the fall of Corregidor — to the no less tragic days when we let our victory in the last war fall from our irresponsible and foolish fingers. All of us will agree that the history of the last twenty-four years can now be seen, in retrospect, to unfold from irremediable negligence to inevitable disaster with the terrible and insistent fatality of a poem by Euripides. All of us will agree that there is no man or group of men of our generation — above all no man or group of men of those who deal with books — who can escape responsibility for the evil which has fallen on our time.

But what needs to be done now is not to look backward and confess our faults; what needs to be done now is to translate this general sense of responsibility into the single and specific responsibilities of single and specific men with single and specific duties. And to translate those specific duties into specific action. It is not enough, for example, for the motion-picture industry to condemn those who assured it two and three and four years ago that its only job was to produce entertainment for the customers, letting death and the raven wheel above the electric signs on the theater marquees. It is necessary now for the motion-picture industry to face the facts and accept the conclusions — to face the fact that the pictures it makes are powerful influences upon the life of this nation; to face the fact that the influence of its pictures will be exerted whether it wishes to exert that influence or not; to face the fact that an escapist picture, a self-deluding picture, exerts an influence as inevitably as a true picture, a picture of actual things — and that its influence is escapist and delusive; to face the fact that the attempt of the industry to evade responsibility for the formation of American opinion by protesting that it had no relation to the formation of opinion — that it was merely engaged in providing entertainment to the American people — is a protest without truth or merit; to face the fact that the motion-picture industry bears a primary and inescapable responsibility, along with the radio and the press and the book trade and the colleges and the schools and all the rest of us, for the failure of the American people to understand long, long before they came to understand it, the nature of the world they lived in and the dangers which that world presented.

There is no such distinction between entertainment on the one side and influence on the other as the motion-picture industry once attempted to draw. The attempt to present the world as it isn't is as much an

action influencing opinion as the attempt to present the
world as it is, and *The Grapes of Wrath* or *The Spanish
Earth* are no more 'propaganda pictures' than the most
illusory of the Hollywood contraptions which conceal
the actualities of a tragic and endangered generation
behind forests of pretty legs and acres of gaudy faces.
If anything, the legs and gaudy faces are the more surely
and more precisely 'propaganda,' for the world — or
rather the non-world — they represent is the world in
which a great part of the American people had drowsily
come to believe — until the bombs fell and the silver
screen was shattered and the mortar and bricks of the
theater itself showed through.

But what is true of the motion-picture industry is
true also of those who concern themselves with books
— and, among them, with those whose concern with
books is their distribution to the men and women who
will read them. The book trade has its share of the responsibility which we all must carry and the book trade,
as much as the motion-picture industry — as much as
the writers and the librarians and the rest — and for
very similar reasons, must accept its share of blame.
The philosophy of distribution adopted during the
twenties and the thirties by the book trade had much
the same effect upon the sale of books as the philosophy
of distribution adopted by the motion-picture industry
had upon the output of motion pictures. The book
trade also — though not so explicitly and not so audibly
— insisted that it was merely engaged in selling merchandise the people wanted and that it accepted therefore no responsibility for the contents of the packages

it sold. Because books were sold in drugstores at cut rates, the men and women who sold them came to think of them in drugstore terms — in cut-rate terms. A book was a three-dollar item or a ninety-eight-cent item and was sold as such. A book was famous because it had sold a hundred thousand copies or five hundred thousand or a million. Department stores stocked books the way they stocked dress-models — and for the same reason — because the customers would buy the model.

What was happening in the book trade, in other words, was about what was happening in the movies. But in the book trade, what was happening was more to be regretted. And for this reason — that the book trade, prior to the twenties, had been an institution which prided itself upon accepting precisely the responsibilities its subsequent practice tended to evade. The book trade had been, indeed, one of the most responsible of all the trades that men could practice. Books, in the last century and the century before, were sold by men who knew them not as packages but as books — men who had, and were entitled to have, opinions about the content and the value of the books they sold — men whose customers came to them, not to learn how many copies of a given novel had been sold before, but to talk about the novel itself — the innards of the novel — the quality of the book.

The tragedy was not so much the trend away from the old-style bookshop — though the trend away from it was sad enough. The tragedy was the decay of a function — a necessary function — a function essential to the dissemination of ideas in books. Books — true books — do not sell themselves. There is nothing about the externals of a true book, not even the most persuasive jacket, to make the readers who should read it want to take it home. True books are sold by the enthusiasm of those who know them and respect them. And that enthusiasm must express itself by word of mouth to count. The most eloquent review by the most esteemed reviewer will do little enough unless reader talks to reader. And of all possible readers, the bookseller who knows his books and knows his customers is the most persuasive talker. Without him the book trade becomes a trade indeed — a trade as impersonal as the trade in soap and soup — a trade of which the only voice is the full-page advertisement and the only measure the dollar-volume of commercial sales.

Until that function — the true bookseller's function — is restored to the selling of books, it is not likely that books will play the part they must play in the shaping of our time, for it is not likely that the books which should reach thousands upon thousands of the citizens of this beleaguered republic will reach a fraction of that number. Books were never more important to this country than they are today. The questions which must be decided, the issues which must be resolved, are, many of them, questions and issues which only books can properly present. The profoundly searching questions, for example, of the order and form of the postwar world are questions for which books and books alone provide an adequate forum. And the basic question — the insistent question — of the true nature of the time in which we live is a question which demands the space and confines of a book. This time has not yet been discovered by the men and women who inhabit it, and only the voyages of the most courageous books will show us what it is.

For many months, therefore — perhaps for many years — books will play a tremendously important, a deeply serious, rôle in the shaping of our history. And not alone the books of economic and political theory. Now as never before in centuries, the true labor of the art of words becomes an essential labor — the labor of the poet who holds experience before us in such a light, in such a posture, that the shape and meaning become visible and ardent — the labor of the novelist who reduces to order and to pattern the confusion and the incoherence of our lives.

The books will be written: have no doubt of that. The need of such a time as this brings out the books of which the time has need. But it is not enough to produce the books. It is not enough to have them reviewed in the columns of the few newspapers and magazines which undertake to review books seriously. It is necessary, if these questions are to be discussed by the vast public which must discuss them — it is necessary that such books as these should reach the hands of those who need them and who know they need them but do not know in practice how to satisfy the need.

Here, then, if ever in the history of the modern world, is a task for the sellers of books — a task which the sellers of books alone can perform — a task which the bulk merchandisers of packaged print can never perform and should never attempt to perform. It is a task moreover which should fire the eye of any man who has the sense of history — a task to which any man could give himself with hope and pride. It is, in other words, precisely the task which the man who loves books and human beings enough to devote his life to mediation between the two will recognize as his.

It involves primarily the conscious acceptance of a difficult and arduous function — a function at once technical and universal — at once professional and human — the function of interpretation between the need of the people of our communities and the literature of our time. To perform it a man must know them both as only the true bookseller can know them. A man must know the books of his time as a scholar knows his titles and he must know the people of his town as a doctor knows his patients. He must know, in other words, what his people need to learn and what his writers have to teach them. And he must bring his people and his books together: not *sub specie aeternitatis* — not under the aspect of eternity — but under the aspect of the time we live in — under this fiery and darkening and yet hopeful sky.

A SUPERSTITION IS DESTROYED

★

★

★

★

A Superstition Is Destroyed

ADDRESS DELIVERED AT THE DIN-
NER IN HONOR OF EDWARD R.
MURROW, CHIEF OF THE EURO-
PEAN STAFF OF THE COLUMBIA
BROADCASTING SYSTEM, DECEM-
BER 2, 1941

IT HAS ALWAYS seemed to me inconsiderate, not to say downright indecent, to talk across a living man as though he were a conscious corpse at his own obsequies.

Therefore I am talking to you, Ed Murrow. And what I have to say to you is this — that you have accomplished one of the great miracles of the world. How much of it was you and how much of it was the medium you used I wouldn't undertake to say — though others have used the medium without the miracle resulting. But however that may be, the fact is that you accomplished it. You destroyed a superstition. You destroyed, in fact, the most obstinate of all the superstitions — the superstition against which poetry and all the arts have fought for centuries — the superstition they too have destroyed. You destroyed the superstition of distance and of time.

I am sorry if I seem to speak in metaphors, for there was never a time when I wished more to speak in literal and precisely meaning words. What I wish to say to you is this: that over the period of your months in London you destroyed in the minds of many men and women in this country the superstition that what is done beyond three thousand miles of water is not really done at all; the ignorant superstition that violence and lies and murder on another continent are not violence and lies and murder here; the cowardly and brutal superstition that the enslavement of mankind in a country where the sun rises at midnight by our clocks is not enslavement by the time we live by; the black and stifling superstition that what we cannot see and hear and touch can have no meaning for us.

How you did this, I repeat I do not know. But that you did was evident to anyone. You spoke, you said, in London. Sometimes you said you were speaking from a roof in London looking at the London sky. Sometimes you said you spoke from underground beneath that city. But it was not in London really that you spoke. It was in the back kitchens and the front living-rooms and the moving automobiles and the hot-

dog stands and the observation cars of another country
that your voice was truly speaking. And what you did
was this: You made real and urgent and present to the
men and women of those comfortable rooms, those safe
enclosures, what these men and women had not known
was present there or real. You burned the city of London in our houses and we felt the flames that burned
it. You laid the dead of London at our doors and we
knew the dead were our dead — were all men's dead —
were mankind's dead — and ours. Without rhetoric,
without dramatics, without more emotion than needed
be, you destroyed the superstition of distance and of
time — of difference and of time.

There were some in this country, Murrow, who did
not want the people of America to hear the things you
had to say. There were some who did not wish to remember that the freedom of speech of which this country is so proud is freedom also to hear — that freedom
to hear is indeed the whole foundation and reason of
freedom to speak. It is not to assure a man the delight
of listening to his own voice that freedom of speech is
guaranteed by the fundamental law of this republic. It
is to assure the people a chance to hear the truth — the
unpleasant truth as well as the reassuring truth; the
dangerous truth as well as the comforting truth.

The right of free speech is guaranteed by a self-
governing people because a self-governing people needs
to know where it is — what it is up against. There are
some in this country — not many but some — who do
not want the American people to know what they are
up against. There are some who attempt to stop the

mouths of those who tell the American people what is happening in their world — who shout 'Warmonger' at those who tell them what is happening in other countries — who shout filthier words than that at those who have seen with their own eyes and who say what they have seen.

But the American people themselves are not afraid to know what they are up against. They were not afraid twenty-five years ago or fifty years before that or ninety years earlier. They were not afraid when you, Murrow, told them the truth about London in the terrible winter of '40-'41. So long as the American people are told and told truly and told candidly what they have to face they will never be afraid. And they will face it.

Because you told them the truth and because you destroyed the superstition of distance and of time which makes the truth turn false you have earned the admiration of your countrymen. This is what I wished to say to you, Murrow. I am grateful for the chance to say it publicly and say it here.

THE COUNTRY OF THE MIND
MUST ALSO ATTACK

★

★

★

★

The Country of the Mind
Must Also Attack

ADDRESS DELIVERED BEFORE THE
AMERICAN LIBRARY ASSOCIATION,
JUNE 26, 1942

IN THE THREE MONTHS from December of last year to February of this the American mentality changed from defensive to offensive and an ultimate victory in the war became, in consequence, a probability instead of a desperate hope. Wars are won by those who mean to win them, not by those who intend to avoid losing them, and victories are gained by those who strike, not by those who parry.

What is true of the people as a whole in the war fought for the domination of the world should be true as well of the intellectuals — the writers and the scholars

and the librarians and the rest — in the war fought for
the countries of the mind. It should be true but isn't.
The intellectuals have learned the first lesson of such
wars: the lesson the nation learned belatedly at Pearl
Harbor. They have learned that their scholar's country
is in real and present danger. They have not yet
learned the second lesson: the lesson the nation learned
in the Dutch East Indies and the Philippines. They
have not yet learned that their scholar's country can be
saved and their world made habitable only by courageous and unrelenting attack.

The learning of the first lesson was long and difficult
enough, as we can all remember. Down through the
thirties to the invasion of Poland a considerable number of American intellectuals preached and practiced an
intellectual isolationism which was at least as frivolous,
and certainly as blind, as the political isolationism of
their political counterparts. They not only denied that
their country of books and scholarship and art and
learning was the principal target of the world revolution then fomented: they denied even that that country
of theirs was in any danger or could possibly be at-
tained or touched by the world-mob gathering against
the sky. Their country, they informed us, was safe beyond its literary seas, its learned waters — safe from any
war or any revolution. Art, they said, and books and
learning of all kinds were things remote from wars, remote from revolutions. All the scholar, or the keeper
of books, or the writer, or the artist, had to do was to
stay on his own side of his particular ocean and tend to
his own affairs and let the wars go by. The wars had

always gone by before, they said, and the art had remained, the books had remained.

Down through the thirties to the invasion of Poland they went on like that. Not all, of course. There were many writers who had looked at Spain and seen what they had seen. There were others who had looked at China. There were scholars who had looked in the books for the things actually lived, the things understood. Not all the American intellectuals of the years before the invasion of Poland were isolationists of the mind, inhabiters beyond imaginary oceans. But many were. And even after Poland there were still many. Until Denmark fell. And Norway fell. And Holland fell. And Belgium fell. And France fell. Then there were none — none but a few ghosts, the shrill inaudible voices.

When you saw in country after country that it was the intellectuals, the artists, the writers, the scholars who were searched out first and shot, or sequestered first, or left to rot first, in the concentration camps — when you saw in country after country that it was the books which were banned or burned or imprisoned, the teachers who were silenced, the publications which were stopped — when you saw all this, it was difficult to insist that the world of art and learning was a world apart from the revolution of our time. It was awkward, not to say embarrassing, to repeat over and over again that the world of books and paintings and philosophy and science was a world set off behind oceans no violence of war could ever cross successfully. It was even a little ridiculous to declare that this attack upon learning —

this attack upon the whole world of the human spirit —
was no affair of those who live by learning and the
spirit — that their only duty was to turn their backs.

So that after the fall of France the first lesson was
learned. What the bombs at Pearl Harbor did to the
political isolationists, the murders of the Gestapo did to
the isolationists of the spirit. It is difficult to argue that
a bomb cannot fall or a man be killed in your country
when the bombs have fallen and the dead men are on
the beaches from Jupiter Light to Quoddy and on north.
It is difficult to argue that the world of art and books
and science is not endangered by a revolution which
has already murdered the artists and the men of letters
and the books.

But the parallel between political isolationism and
intellectual isolationism, though it holds in part, does
not hold in full. Political isolationism in the United
States was replaced by a defensive mentality, which was
replaced in time by a mentality committed to attack.
Intellectual isolationism was replaced by a defensive
mentality only: the second transformation never followed. Scholars and writers admitted after Czechoslo-
vakia and France and Norway that their country — the
country of the mind — the country of the free man's
mind — was indeed under attack and that their pretense
of inviolability, of other-worldliness, was a pretense as
unrealistic as it was unworthy. They admitted indeed
that their country, the country they inhabited as
scholars and as writers and as men of books, was the
principal target of the revolution of our time — that
this revolution was in fact as in word a revolution

aimed against the intellect, against the mind, against the things of the mind — a revolution of ignorance and violence and superstition against the city of truth. They agreed in consequence that the city must be held, must be defended. But the second step, the second and essential step, the scholars and the men of letters have not taken even yet. They have not accepted the necessity of offensive war. They have not perceived that the defense of the country of the mind involves an affirmation, an assertion of a fighting and affirmative belief in intellectual things, a willingness not only to resist attacks upon their world and on themselves but to conceive offensives of their own and fight them through and win them.

A very large number of American writers have enlisted in one way or another in the war against fascism — some as soldiers, some as polemical writers, some as employees of the government. Scholars have put their scholarship at the service of their country and their country's cause, artists and musicians also. But it is in their capacity as citizens of the political, not of the intellectual, world that these men have acted. They have put aside their quality as writers and scholars for the duration of the war. They have said, in effect: 'Our scholar's world, our writer's world is threatened: we will defend it on the political front, the front of arms — we will defend the city of the mind by defending the actual cities of our other world, the world we know as citizens and men.'

It is a courageous thing to do and a necessary thing to do. The actual cities must be held and the physical

battles for their safety must be fought and won at any
cost, at any sacrifice. Certainly the enlistment of the
scholars in those battles is a heartening and an admirable thing, just as the failure of men of scholarship
and letters to oppose the rising fascist revolution in the
thirties was a shame to western scholarship and a re-
proach our generation will not soon forget. But
courageous and necessary as these actions are, they are
nevertheless inadequate to the scholar's obligations.
Whatever may be true of other cities, the city of the
mind cannot be defended by deserting it to fight on
other fronts. Above all, it cannot be defended by deserting it when the ultimate objective of the forces
which have made this war is precisely the destruction
of that city.

To fail to understand that fact is to fail to understand the nature of the conflict in which our world is
now engaged. This conflict is not a conflict which can
be won by arms alone, for it is not a conflict fought for
things which arms alone can conquer. It is a conflict
fought for men's convictions — for the things which lie
beneath convictions — for ideas. The war of arms
might end in victory on the Pacific and along the Chan-
nel and in the Mediterranean and in Africa and Asia,
and the war might still be lost if the battles of belief
are lost — above all if the battle to maintain the power
and authority of truth and free intelligence were lost —
if the confidence of men in learning and in reason and
in truth were broken and replaced by trust in force and
ignorance and superstition — if the central battle for the
preservation of the ultimate authority of mind in human living shall be lost.

And that central battle can be lost. We shall deceive ourselves if we pretend that the attack upon intellectual things, the attack upon the things of art and of the spirit which has been a fundamental part of the maneuvers of our adversaries, has been unimportant in effect. On the contrary, no single element of their propaganda has been more successful than the propaganda the fascists have brought against the intellectual authority. And for an excellent reason. Which is this: that fascism is in its essence a revolt of man against himself — a revolt of stunted, half-formed, darkened men against a human world beyond their reach, and most of all against the human world of reason and intelligence and sense.

No propaganda was or could have been more powerful than the anti-intellectual propaganda of the fascists, because no propaganda responded more precisely to the prejudices and the emotional predispositions of those to whom the fascist revolution made its principal appeal. The bankrupt merchants, the frustrated apprentices, the disappointed junior engineers, the licked, half-educated, unsuccessful clerks and journalists and discharged soldiers to whom the fascist revolution called in every country where the fascist cause made headway, were men sick of a profound, a deadly sickness — a sickness they had caught in the swarming, crowded, fetid and unlovely air of the swarming and unlovely time which bore them — a sickness of which the name was ignorance and envy. For men whom ignorance and envy bred no conceivable propaganda was more seductive than the propaganda which presented all learning, all enlightenment, all distinction of the man and mind as false and foolish.

For a generation to which the world had ceased to make either sense or loveliness or justice, a propaganda which belittled human intelligence and sneered at human morality was a propaganda which was believed before it was uttered. Defeated by a world which used them as tools but had no use for them as men, they turned, not on the world but on themselves — on man — on all those things in man which seemed to men before them to be admirable and of good repute but now to them seemed otherwise. The fascist propaganda which tore down the intellectual authority, the moral rule, was not, in other words, *one* of the devices of the fascist revolution — it *was* the fascist revolution. For fascism is in essence nothing but the latest, saddest, most pathetic, and most hopeless form of the ancient revolution of mankind against itself — the recurring and always tragic effort of mankind to kill the best it knows in order to make peace with what is not the best — but would be if the best were dead.

It would be foolish therefore — indeed it would be worse than foolish — to pretend to ourselves that the attack upon our scholar's world is not a dangerous attack — an attack which has done injury already and can still do more. But certainly we have no temptation to belittle its effect. We know what harm has been done in other countries and in this as well. We know, for example, if we read the press or watch the signs in any medium, how deep the effort to destroy the confidence of men in learning and in intellectual things has gone.

There was never a time, I think, in the history of this country when learning was held cheaper than it is to-day — or when the men of learning and of letters had less honor. A hundred and fifty years ago in America, or a hundred years ago, or fifty, a man of learning was honored for his learning. Today to be an intellectual is to be an object of suspicion in the public mind. To be a professor is to invite attack in any public service, any public undertaking. To be an artist is to live beyond the reach of serious consideration.

There is no occasion to produce testimony or to document the obvious. The evidence is so generally familiar that it passes without comment. When an attempt was made in an ill-attended session of the House of Representatives this last spring to cut the appropriation of the Library of Congress to such a point that the national library of the United States would have been unable to buy new books beyond its regular continuations and subscriptions — an attempt which might have succeeded had not the House and Senate by common and non-partisan action reversed its initial success — when this attack was made upon a great symbol of learning, a great institution of scholarship, no public outcry was aroused. No public resentment was expressed even by those who might most readily have voiced resentment. There were two editorials, one each in the *New York Times* and in the *Washington Star*. And we — such is the humility of those these days who have the charge of learning — we were grateful for these two. And did what could be done with their support.

This angers you, my friends, to hear of now. It did

not anger you then. And why? Because you never
heard of it, most likely. And why did you never hear
of it? Because neither to your friends, nor to your newspapers nor to your radio commentators, did it seem to
have significance enough to call it to your notice. And
why? The answer I think is obvious: it was not news.
It was not news that an attack had been made upon an
institution of learning: such attacks had been made before and frequently. It was not news that the leader of
the attack had unconsciously revealed a fear of books,
a fear of letting information reach the people, a fear of
scholarship and learning: such fears had been revealed
before, and not least often by the very man the *Times*
rebuked. Nothing in the sorry spectacle was news to
anyone. Fifty years ago an attack upon a great library,
an attempt to deprive the people of this country of their
books, would have brought down upon the politician
who attempted it a storm of criticism in the public
press. Today it passes almost without comment.

But no citations of the evidence are necessary. You
know the record for yourselves. You know what headway the propaganda aimed against the intellectuals has
made. You know where you stand in this conflict —
you and everything you care for. You know therefore
whether it is possible to maintain, as we and others like
us have maintained so long, a negative position, a defensive mind.

For myself I do not think so. The city of learning
— or so it seems to me — can be defended in this war
only as the city of freedom can be defended: by attack.
To realize that the world of books and learning and of

art is the principal objective of those who would destroy our time, and to sit back in a humble and defensive silence awaiting whatever onslaught they wish next
to make, is the rôle, it seems to me, not only of cowardice but of foolishness as well. Like this America we
love enough to fight for overseas on every continent, our
scholar's country is a country we must fight abroad to
save. Not by awaiting attack but by preventing it, not
by resisting but by overcoming, can the towering city
of the mind be victor in this war. And unless we are
ready now or very soon to bring the battle to our
enemies and overcome them — to strike down ignorance
where ignorance appears — to fly our flag of truth and
reason higher than our enemies can cut it down — we
cannot win this war within the war on which the outcome of the war itself depends.

★

★

★

★

The Image of Victory

PRESENTED AS THE STEARNS
LECTURE AT PHILLIPS ACADEMY
IN ANDOVER, MAY 15, 1942

THIS WAR PRESENTS a curious paradox: a curious division of minds precisely at the point at which the minds of men engaged in war are commonly united. Men engaged in war are commonly agreed on one thing at least — the victory they mean to win. We are not altogether agreed on that point. We are determined that we shall win a victory. But what victory we do not altogether know. We have the will to victory. But the idea of victory, the conception of victory, eludes us.

I do not wish to be misunderstood. I am not discussing the morale of the American people. The

morale of the American people — whatever that ambiguous and patronizing word may mean — is excellent.
If I have any knowledge of American opinion — and
I think I have access to such knowledge as there is —
the American people are considerably sounder in their
opinions than most of those who worry about American
opinion seem to think. They have resisted, over the
past eighteen months, the efforts of powerful sections of
the press to fool them with defeatist and divisionist
propaganda of the noisiest and most expensive kind,
and they can be trusted, I believe, to go on resisting
defeatist and divisionist propaganda for a long time to
come.

Neither, when I speak of a disagreement about the
nature of American victory, the victory of the United
Nations, do I have in mind the special cases, the sick
souls, the defeated men. There is an insignificant minority of Americans, as there was also a minority of
Frenchmen and Norwegians and Yugoslavs and Danes,
who do not want an American victory — who fear the
victory of a democratic people, in the long democratic
revolution of which Henry Wallace has so movingly
spoken, more than they fear a democratic defeat. We
know what they are and why. In the mirror of France
we know them very well. Their name is Laval and
Doriot and Darlan. They need neither our consideration nor our very great concern: only our watchfulness
and sharpened scorn.

What I am considering here is something much more
important, both for now and for the years after. What
I have in mind is the honest apprehension, the loyal

doubt, the understandable anxiety of those who are determined we shall win this war; who are willing, if need be, to die to help their people win it; but who are nevertheless unable to understand clearly, or to imagine precisely, what our victory in this war will be. Specifically, what I have in mind is the understandable confusion of a generation of young men who were brought up to believe that the last war, though won, was lost, and that the war in which we are now engaged is nothing but the last war fought again; who therefore and most reasonably ask each other and ask us what victory this war can truly win — what victory other than the negative, defensive victory we won before, or won and lost before, or only lost.

Those who ask this question understand very well what *defeat* in this war would mean. Indeed it would be impossible for them not to understand. The evidence is before them everywhere they look — in the starvation and misery and death of Poland, in the death and starvation and slavery of Greece, in the French prisons at the first light when the volley rattles and the hostages chosen by lot, picked out of their cells by lot, and by lot lined up in the half-light, and by lot shot down, are murdered. What they do not understand is victory. Victory as the mere absence of defeat is something they do not wish to think about. They know that kind of victory and how it tastes. But victory as victory — victory as an affirmative thing — they cannot easily imagine. Victory as an affirmative thing means something won. A disarmed enemy is not something won: a disarmed enemy is merely something prevented.

And so too of a world order to assure peace in the future: a world order to assure peace is also something prevented — in the future. These things are desirable. They are valuable. We should have secured them twenty years ago. But are they victory? Are they the sum and substance of the victory we mean to win?

It is an understandable question, and those who ask it have every reason to ask. They will not be answered by words which tell them that Naziism and all its works are evil. They know Naziism and all its works are evil and they mean to destroy both it and them. Neither will they be answered by talk about our cause — talk which says our cause is freedom and freedom is a cause worth fighting for in any country. They know very well that freedom is our cause. They know that freedom was never more clearly the cause of any people than it is ours: that despotism and tyranny were never more cynically avowed by any enemy than by the enemy which threatens us. They believe also that freedom is worth fighting for. They mean to fight for it. They mean to win also. But nevertheless they are not satisfied.

And they are right not to be satisfied.

They have proposed to themselves an end and they mean to attain that end, but they cannot conceive it. They feel themselves moving at an uncontrollable speed and by their own will, their own effort, toward an end, a goal, they cannot in any way imagine. They intend to gain a victory — but what victory? What will it mean to them? What will it mean to any man? The misery, the economic dislocation, the inane prosperity followed by the meaningless hunger of the victory we won before? Or something else? And, if so, what else? Land? Islands? They cannot imagine the usefulness of land or islands. Empire? It is difficult to talk these days of empires. They think of victory in the future: they think of empires in the past. They have no patience with those who talk of empires or of islands now. They wish to know how they are to imagine their victory in terms they can believe in and understand.

It is this that people mean when they ask their leaders to tell them what we are fighting for. They do not mean that they wish to be told *why* we are fighting. They know very well why we are fighting. They always knew the why of this fighting even when the appeasers and the isolationists and the opportunists and the plain moral cowards were telling them they need never fight — that the fighting was no concern of theirs. Neither do they mean that they wish to be told what we are fighting *against*. They have had no doubt what we were fighting against from the first shot of the first gun in Poland. Some of them knew before that, in Spain and in other countries. What they mean is precisely what they say: they wish to know what we are fighting *for* — what we propose to bring to pass by our fighting. Now that we are engaged in this war; now that we are engaged against enemies we know and for reasons we understand; now that we are engaged in this war and intend to fight this war — what do we propose to win *from* it and *by* it?

It is an understandable question but it is, nevertheless, a curious question — a question which reflects the doubtful and still confusing experiences of the last twenty-five years, and particularly of the years which followed the last war. Even the young men who ask this question most, and who most have right to ask it, speak out of the confusion and bewilderment of that experience. They have the sense of change in their bones and in their blood, but they have in their heads the shadows and the disappointments of their fathers' years. They trust themselves but not their time, and therefore they question their time. They are right, I think, to question it. But I doubt that the answer they are looking for is as far off as they sometimes think.

Certainly it is not as far off as the answers they are sometimes given would lead them to believe. And for this reason: that the answers they are given are, for the most part, answers not as to the meaning of their victory but as to the structure of the world their victory will make possible. The answers, in other words, are answers about that far-off unreal country called the 'post-war world' — the world the economists and the statesmen and the technicians will construct out of the rubble of the pre-war world when the victory is won. But it is not this, I think, the young men wish to know. They are not concerned, most of them — they are not concerned yet — with the economy or the international organization of the world which will follow their victory. They wish to know — certainly they wish to know — whether they will return to tramp the streets for jobs as their fathers did. They wish to know whether they will have to fight their war a second time in their forties and their fifties as their fathers, they believe, are now

obliged to fight a second time the war they won. But
before they come to these things — before they come to
the economic order or the international controls — they
wish to understand what their victory itself will be.
They wish to see the shape of their victory as the Greeks,
who made shapes of victory out of stone, once saw it.
They wish to believe in their victory as itself a creative
and accomplishing thing.

I do not think it is impossible for them to see this or
believe in it. On the contrary, it would seem to me that
the answer they require is already in their mouths. If
they will trust themselves, if they will trust their own
sense of the changing time, if they will look ahead and
not back, they will give themselves their answer. For if
anything about this war is certain, it is this: that those
who win this war will win the future of the world.

They will win it not in some metaphorical or poetic
sense, but in the most precise and practical meaning of
the term. They will win the future of the world to such
an extent that they will be able to change not its gov-
ernments only, but its geography, its actual shape and
meaning in men's minds. And they will win it not for
now, not for a generation, but, if they have the courage
and the will, for all the future men can now foresee.
Whatever the Nazis may say about *Lebensraum,* whatever their Far-Eastern accomplices may say about
Greater-Asia Co-Prosperity Spheres, whatever our own
imperialists may say about a new imperium, it is not
for continents or islands or for seas between them that
this war is fought. This war is fought on the one side
to dominate, on the other side to liberate, an age — a

new age, an age which every man who lets his eyes look forward can now see.

The sense of the new age, the new world, has troubled men for generations. They have had the sense of the future in them a long time. Change after change in the machinery of their lives has thrown their minds forward. For the most part they have been deceived. The changes have proved, for the most part, to be changes on the surface only; changes of convenience or of habit; water out of a tap instead of water out of a well; power out of a steam kettle instead of power out of a mule; light from a wire instead of light from wax. But the sense of the future has haunted them nevertheless. And now the sense of the future has come true. They see before them — those who have eyes to see — a world so different, different in so clear a sense, that they have no choice but to accept its difference.

Most of us thought of the airplane in the years between the wars as a new gadget — an automobile which flew. We had been confused by a long list of inventions, each more spectacular than the last, of which the airplane was the latest. Even when this war began, we did not understand its meaning. We told each other that after the war there would be thousands of planes as there were millions of cars after the last war, and everyone would have his own. The plane was simply another gadget in a gadget universe, a new convenience. We do not think that now. We know now that the plane is capable of altering the geography of our world — and therefore the history of our world. We know that the world which the airplane dominates will be a

different world from the world which went before. We
see before us, in other words — or we can see it if we
look — an age new in its essential possibilities and
therefore a new age.

The ages of human history are not created by mechanical inventiveness, but there have been, in the history
of our race, mechanical inventions which have changed
the possibilities, and thus the minds, and thus, for better or for worse, the men. Landlocked men thought
of the earth as a huge island surrounded by an unknown, undiscoverable sea. Seafaring men, as they extended their laborious mastery of the water, attempted
to think of the earth as a globe, but succeeded only in
imagining it as a belt of traversable water and inhab-
itable land fenced off between the two impenetrable
polar caps of ice and fog and cold — a globe in theory,
but in fact a globe-encircling river with temperate or
tropic shores. That the mastery of the air will fix a
different image in men's minds — an image which will
father a new age — no one who knows the meaning of
that mastery can doubt — no one who knows what
voyages men and planes have made already in this war:
the long flights of the ferrying command, the bombing
thrusts at unbelievable objectives, the regular runs from
continent to continent.

Indeed the image is already forming. To men of
my generation, born in a seafaring world, the port of
Murmansk lies east across the Atlantic and on east
around the Scandinavian peninsula, thousands of sea
miles. But Murmansk, to the fliers, is a bare eleven
hundred miles north across the polar ice cap from

Greenland. To us Greenland is farther east than New
York City and therefore farther than New York from
Tokyo. To the airmen, New York to Tokyo is seven
thousand miles; Greenland to Tokyo around the pole
five thousand. To us the straight line from La Guardia
Field to Foynes in Ireland is north of east, straight out
across the Atlantic. To them the shortest line, but not
the straightest — for no distances along the globe are
straight — curves north along the edge of Newfound-
land, along the curving of the earth, and on around.

No one can doubt that the world which mastery of
the air creates will be a different world. But the nature
of that world — its human character — is still uncertain.
And it is that nature which the outcome of this war will
fix. One or the other, the Nazi image of the airmen's
earth or ours, will be imposed upon the world that follows. We know them both: the Nazi image because
the Nazis have spelled it out for us a hundred times;
our own because already we begin to see its outlines.
We can guess even now what the image of the airmen's
earth will be if free men make it. If those who have
the mastery of the air are free men and imagine
for themselves as free men what their world could be,
their world will be the full completed globe — the final
image men have moved toward for so long and never
reached.

Never in all their history have men been able truly
to conceive the world as one: a single sphere, a globe
having the qualities of a globe, a round earth in which
all the directions eventually meet, in which there is no
center because every point, or none, is center — an

equal earth which all men occupy as equals. The airmen's earth, if free men make it, will be truly round: a
globe in practice, not in theory. Already, under the
compulsions of the war, a generation of young men has
come to think in terms of globes. It is with strings on
globes, not rulers on navigating charts, that the officers
of the ferrying command plot out their distances, and it
is always with the curving of the earth in mind that the
young pilots of the bombing commands imagine to
themselves their flights. The obstacles which limited
the earth to men in ships are not obstacles to men in
planes. Cold to the airmen is no barrier: they find it
everywhere and occupy it in all climates. Ice to the
airmen is no wall: they cross it easily as land or water.
Distance is no hindrance. The limited voyages of even
the greatest ships were voyages across a seeming-level
sea. The great flights of the bomber planes and the
ferry planes of this war are flights *around* the earth,
not across it. The famous clipper which was caught
by the war in Australian waters and made its way *west*
to New York: the two ships which flew into Moscow
with the Hopkins mission and returned, one east and
one west, to meet on an American air field — the men
who flew these ships were men who had the sense of
the roundness of the earth as no men could have had it
before the air was mastered.

If we win this war — if we and the free peoples united
with us win this war — the image of the age which now
is opening will be this image of a global earth, a completed sphere. But if the Nazis win, the image will be
very different. The air-earth as the Nazis see it is not

the earth swept forward to the final and completed
sphere, but the earth thrown backward to the ancient
landlocked island of the centuries before the seas were
opened. The official Nazi architects of this official
Nazi air-earth are the Nazi geopoliticians — the professors and the generals of the Haushofer school of generals and geographers. To the Nazi geopoliticians, the
true picture of the world is not the picture of a globe,
but of a 'world island' with a 'heart land' at its center.
The 'heart land' is Germany. The 'world island' is the
vast land-linked mass of Europe, Africa, and Asia.
Around this island are the seven seas. And anchored
off the island shores in tributary dependence to the iron
Main are all the other continents and islands of the
earth — the Americas, Australia, Greenland, all the rest.
From the Nazi 'heart land,' air power will dominate the
'world island.' From the shores of the 'world island,'
air power will dominate the seas — as air power dom-
inated the seas off Malaya and the Pacific archipelagos.
Across the seas the threat of air power will hold the
tributary continents and islands in subjection. It is not,
I assure you, a dream. It is a geography. It is a geography which has worked in the Eastern Mediterranean
and the Southwest Pacific and which the Nazis mean
shall work for the whole earth.

If the Nazis win, in other words, the new age of air
power will be the old landlocked age of mythological
men, and the image of the airmen's earth will be the
image of the central island and the encircling sea. It
is curious to recall, in this context, that there was some
talk and more writing a year or two ago about the Nazi

New Order as an order new not in name only but in
truth.   It is curious to remember that some who loved
the air and knew the air accepted for themselves and
even taught this theory.   For surely, whatever else the
Nazi New Order may be — and there are millions of
living and half-living and no longer living Frenchmen,
Dutchmen, Poles, Norwegians who could tell us what
it is — whatever else the Nazi New Order may be, it is
not the new order of the airmen's age.   It is indeed the
precise opposite of that order: the denial and suppression so complete and so brutal that a man might wonder
whether the Nazis had not fought this war precisely for
that purpose, precisely to use the mastery of the air as
an instrument to abort the promise of that mastery;
promise that to them was threat.

It is against this Nazi New Order of death, and new
revelation of old ignorance, that this war is fought.   But
not *against* them only.   Those who think it is — those
who think of this war as a negative, defensive war;
those who question what our victory in this war can be
— have not considered very carefully the nature of the
time we live in: the opening, eventful nature of this
time.   They have not considered that there lies ahead
of us, by every certainty, an opening age, and that that
age belongs by right of its own logic to the free — to us
and to all free men.   They have not realized that in
preventing our enemies from conquering that age and
distorting that age we must conquer it ourselves; that in
driving out and forever forbidding those who would
have seized the future, we will seize it; that in destroying by force of arms the suppressive and tyrannical

image the Nazis would have stamped upon it, we must inevitably stamp an image of our own. So far indeed is it from being true that the nature of our victory is difficult to name, that no man who considers what the struggle truly is can fail to name it. We who win this war will win the right and power to impose upon the opening age the free man's image of the earth we live in. We who win this war will win the future. The future which will follow from this war belongs to us.

Neither mastery of the air nor power in the air nor the airmen's global image of the earth can make, alone, the world we hope to live in. There are no panaceas and no cures, and the future of any people is a continuation of its past — a hope shackled by history. Nevertheless we know, all of us, the power of images in our lives and in the lives of nations. We know that those who think their world a free place of free movement, of free commerce both in men and words, are already free men, whatever limitations are put upon their freedom by brutality or force. We know also that those who do not think of their world in this way, who accept another image of their world, are slaves however they hold themselves, or however they move in apparent freedom from one place to another. We know therefore what it means to win this war.

For hundreds of years, thousands of years, the sea was the great symbol of freedom, and men struggled in many wars over many centuries to keep it so. To be free was to go on the sea waters. There was no man, said the ancient Saxon poet, but 'longing comes upon him to fare forth on the water.' It was the same with the Greeks and with all ancient peoples. The sea was freedom. The sea was the great symbol of freedom. Men, once they had built ships and learned the winds, would fare forth on the water. They would go and come freely; trade back and forth; exchange cloth and grain and iron; exchange words; exchange beliefs; discover new continents. For two thousand, three thousand years it was the opening endless sea which men followed for their freedom.

Now there is a new element upon which men can fare forth. Men have mastered the air. And the question now — the question, whether we so intend or not, on which this terrible war is fought — is whether the air will be a new symbol and a new practice of an even greater freedom, or whether it will not; whether the air will be to the sea what the sea was to the locked land, or whether it will not; whether the air will be an instrument of freedom such as men have never dared to dream of or an instrument of slavery such as men had never thought to feel — an instrument of slavery by which a single nation can enslave the earth and hold the earth in slavery without the hope or possibility of rebellion and revolt.

To win this war for freedom is not to win a doubtful victory. To win this war for freedom is to win the greatest triumph any nation, any people, ever won.

THE WESTERN SKY

A Poem

★

★

★

★

The Western Sky
Words for a Song

TO ROY HARRIS

Stand Stand against the rising night
O freedom's land, O freedom's air:
Stand steep and keep the fading light
That eastward darkens everywhere.

Hold Hold the golden light and lift
Hill after hill-top, one by one —
Lift up America O lift
Green freedom to the evening sun.

Lift up your hills till conquered men
Look westward to their blazing height.

Lift freedom till its fire again
Kindles the countries of the night.

Be proud America to bear
The endless labor of the free —
To strike for freedom everywhere
And everywhere bear liberty.

Lift up O land O land lift clear
The lovely signal of your skies.
If freedom darkens eastward, here
Here on the west let freedom rise.